Reader's Digest
Wildlife Watch

Gardens & Parks in Autumn

Reader's Digest
Wildlife Watch

Gardens & Parks in Autumn

Published by
The Reader's Digest Association Limited
London • New York • Sydney • Montreal

Contents

Wildlife habitats and havens

Park watch

Animals and plants in focus

Garden watch

Introduction

September is the softest month, coaxing mushrooms from the damp earth, ripening green to gold, swelling fruit with warm rain. After the dusty days of high summer, with their hard light and withering heat, the gentle touch of early autumn stirs life from the land. Animals that remained hidden from the burning summer sun begin to appear by day, sheltered by lingering mists and dew-soaked grass. Frogs and toads, intent on finding prey, forage in the green shade beneath foliage refreshed by overnight rain. Snails and slugs emerge from their refuges to glide over the damp ground in search of food, and at night earthworms push up through the softened soil to gather fallen leaves and haul them down into their burrows. Parks and gardens seem to revive as tattered petals drop away to reveal glossy hips and sweet berries, while hard capsules split and burst to release the plumed seeds of willowherb and thistledown.

◀ The majestic horse chestnut tree that often grows in parkland is among the first to change colour in autumn. The first frosts turn its big compound leaves yellow and brown, and soon they are drifting to the ground.

▲ Moisture-loving snails, such as the strawberry snail – a garden specialist – relish the damp days of autumn. They are preyed upon by thrushes, hedgehogs and frogs.

▲ Among the easiest of ducks to identify – in the case of males, at least – tufted ducks gather in large numbers on many big park lakes to moult once the breeding season is over.

Nectar and fruit

Although fewer flowers bloom in the borders and wild corners, many gardens are alive with the buzz and flash of nectar-feeding bees and butterflies. The flattened, pale violet heads of late-flowering sedums lure them in droves, to probe and sip sweet nectar with their delicate tongues. They are joined by a glinting army of small beetles and flies, including the striped hoverflies (see pages 66–67) that are so often mistaken for stinging wasps. There are wasps in evidence, too. Released from nursery duties as their breeding colonies break up, they roam in search of nectar and ripe fruit rather than the insects that they gathered throughout the summer. Irresistibly attracted by the scent of sugar or fruit juice, they disrupt many a garden lunch or parkland picnic. The swags of autumn-flowering ivy that festoon old walls and fences often swarm with them, making the ivy hum as if electrically charged.

Where there are insects, there are spiders. The garden spider population seems to explode in September, but in reality their webs just become more obvious when they are spangled with overnight dew.

These orb-web builders ensnare many insect victims, but many more are captured by other web-building, ambushing, hunting and jumping spiders that lurk among the vegetation (see pages 68–72).

In turn, both insects and spiders are seized by birds intent on building up their energy reserves in preparation for the coming winter. Tiny, russet wrens work their way through low shrubs in search of prey, occasionally bursting out to dart low over the ground to the next bush. In parkland trees, blue tits dangle precariously at the ends of slender, swaying branches as they check the foliage and developing buds, while mouse-like treecreepers (see pages 94–97) spiral up the trunks probing the bark for small invertebrates.

Migrants and hibernators

In the sky overhead, wheeling swallows and house martins (see pages 50–55) trawl for tiny flies borne up by the air. These dedicated insect-eaters have a different agenda, for when their prey becomes scarce they will migrate to the tropics to find another source of food and they must eat to prepare for the journey. They start to gather on overhead wires in August in

▲ The frosts of late autumn can create magical effects. Here the foliage of tufted hair grass has been transformed into a glittering fountain of ice.

▶ Most moths disappear in late autumn, but the mottled umber is one of a few species that stays active throughout the winter. The winged males can be seen from September to March.

▶ The sharp 'tchick' calls of great spotted woodpeckers are often heard in autumn parkland as young adults hatched the previous spring bicker over territory. The red nape patch of this bird shows that it is a male.

readiness for the long flight south, and the departure of the last flocks in October is a sure sign that the afterglow of summer has finally faded.

More omnivorous birds have no need to take such drastic action, because they can switch between foods to take advantage of whatever is available. Blackbirds and song thrushes feast on windfall apples lying on lawns, while garden robins supplement their insect diet with ripe blackberries and elderberries, spreading the plants' seeds in their droppings in the process. Up in parkland trees, the acrobatic nuthatch (see pages 102–105) takes insects and spiders or nuts and seeds as the opportunity arises, often wedging nuts into bark crevices to hack into them with its strong bill. Meanwhile, ground-feeding finches, such as the chaffinch (see pages 62–65), feast on scattered seed, working their way over the grass in inconspicuous flocks, while starlings (see pages 56–61) and rooks probe the softened ground for buried insect grubs.

The feverish activity of the birds is matched by that of more secretive creatures, such as the nocturnal hedgehog and edible dormouse (see pages 42–47). Their winter survival strategy is very different, however, since they deal with the twin problems of food shortage and low temperatures by slipping into the torpid state known as hibernation. This is not just deep sleep – the animal abandons the attempt to keep warm, and allows its body temperature to fall well below the level needed for active life. In this state, it uses very little energy, so it does not need to eat, but it does need to build up reserves of energy-rich fat in advance. So for hedgehogs and dormice, autumn is a time of urgent activity as they prepare for hibernation (see pages 16–17). They must eat as much as possible, taking advantage of the warm weather while it lasts. Bats have the same schedule to meet, and the night skies above parks and gardens are scenes of invisible aerial hunting as the bats eat their fill of night-flying moths, beetles and flies.

Seasonal symbols

Meanwhile, garden fungi are sprouting in the wet, but still warm, soil (see pages 73–76). These strange organisms, neither plant nor animal, are stirred into action by the mild autumn weather. Underground fibres clump together to form nodes that push up through the soil and expand into mushrooms and toadstools, which scatter their spores on the wind. They can appear overnight, then linger for a few days before collapsing or shrivelling away. They are symbolic of autumn, both of its fruitfulness and of its transience. Even more symbolic, however, are the dead leaves that drift down from deciduous trees

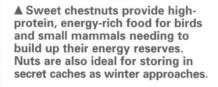

▲ Sweet chestnuts provide high-protein, energy-rich food for birds and small mammals needing to build up their energy reserves. Nuts are also ideal for storing in secret caches as winter approaches.

◀ A crop of berries on an ornamental shrub may attract a nomadic flock of waxwings that have flown south from Scandinavia. Scarce and unpredictable, they usually feed for a few days and then disappear.

▲ The pipistrelle bat frequents gardens and parks. There are two species and in southern England they can be seen hunting tiny flies in the night sky until late November.

to carpet the ground and bury the last vestige of summer. In woodlands of oak, ash and birch these fallen leaves form drifts of muted browns, greys and yellows, but in parks the native autumn russets are punctuated by the vivid reds and oranges of exotic maples, hickories and planes. Thousands of visitors are drawn to Westonbirt Arboretum in Gloucestershire to experience the spectacular autumn colour of its world-famous maple collection (see pages 34–39). Similar delights can be found in many local parks.

First frost

Throughout the mushroom season of early autumn many tender, exotic garden plants keep growing and flowering. Then one night the temperature dips below freezing, and dawn reveals the first frost. Initially, the damage may seem light, but within hours dahlias and canna lilies start to blacken and collapse, their tissues destroyed by the ice crystals that have ruptured their cells. If their roots are not protected from further frosts, they are likely to die, but many native plants and their garden cultivars are more resilient. Their foliage dies back to ground level, but their root systems survive, and will sprout again in spring.

The dieback of these herbaceous perennials is less spectacular than the autumn leaf fall, but it marks an equally profound turning point in the year. This is when most of the insects disappear, either dying or slipping into their winter refuges (see pages 28–29). The hibernating mammals vanish, too, along with cold-blooded creatures such as frogs, toads, snakes and lizards, which have no option but to lie dormant through the cold months ahead. They retreat to the depths of garden compost heaps or the piles of fallen leaves swept up in parks, and creep into crevices in logpiles and rockeries.

Many apparently vulnerable animals remain active. Tiny wood mice and bank voles gather seeds and berries, carrying them into their burrows as insurance against the food shortages to come. Grey squirrels collect nuts and acorns, often using considerable ingenuity to raid supposedly squirrel-proof birdfeeders (see pages 48–49). By night, the brown rat emerges to look for food, which in the rat's case means virtually anything edible (see pages 84–89). Winter-visiting birds arrive from the far north. Mixed flocks of fieldfares and redwings – relatives of the native thrushes and blackbird – descend on holly and hawthorn, and hungrily strip the berries after their long flight from Scandinavia. Ducks start to mass on park lakes, the males already resplendent in breeding plumage. Then one morning the surface of the lake is a sheet of ice, and winter has arrived.

▲ In September the white flowers of guelder rose give way to bright red, luscious-looking berries that are eagerly eaten by birds, such as thrushes and blackbirds.

▲ Yellow clusters of sulphur tuft are often mistaken for the parasitic honey fungus, but this is a harmless species that often grows on dead wood in parkland. The clumps can be well over 20cm (8in) across.

▶ The wood mouse often visits gardens, and can sometimes be seen climbing through shrubs in search of seeds and fruits. It may eat these on the spot, or carry them off to eat later.

Wildlife habitats and havens

- Autumn wild flower garden
- Preparing for hibernation
- Garden hedges
- Wildlife in puddles and pools
- Urban buildings – useful shelters
- Autumn retreats
- Autumn park activity
- Westonbirt Arboretum – spectacular colours

Autumn wild flower garden

Plants that flourish late in the year in the wild can provide a last burst of colour in the garden, as well as vital nectar for late-flying butterflies.

Sea aster

Once confined to coastal regions, sea asters still grow mainly on the shores of estuaries, in salt marshes and on sea cliffs. However, these plants are also increasingly found inland alongside main roads, where the salt used for de-icing in winter spreads on to the verges to create soils like those found in a salt marsh.

Sea asters have fleshy leaves for storing water, and daisy-like flowers with bluish purple petals (sometimes absent) and yellow centres. The flowers appear from July to October, making cultivated varieties colourful autumn additions to the garden.

▶ Sea asters grow readily among stones and pebbles in a rock garden, which resembles their natural habitat, but they also do well on alkaline soils inland.

▲ Canadian goldenrod grows wild in a wide range of settings and climates, including upland and northern areas. In the garden, larger plants are best placed at the back of a border.

Goldenrod

In the 16th century goldenrod was well known for its healing properties, and made into either an ointment or a hot drink. The Latin name of the genus to which it belongs, *Solidago*, means 'to make whole'.

There are several species and various hybrid forms, many of which have been specially bred. Canadian goldenrod is an adaptable perennial that takes root in rocky soil or hedge banks and produces curving golden plumes of flowers that rise above narrow leaves between July and September.

Late flowering makes goldenrod a popular autumn garden plant, although it seeds so prolifically that it can become a nuisance. Some plants can grow to 2.5m (8ft 2in) tall, and may require staking in exposed gardens.

Michaelmas daisy

A complex group of at least six species, Michaelmas daisies are native to eastern North America. The plants were introduced to Britain three centuries ago and soon became naturalised in the wild, forming a wide variety of colourful hybrids.

Michaelmas daisies are perennial plants and produce drifts of flowers each year that range from pale blue to deep mauve, both in gardens and in the wild. They often occur in waste areas and especially along railway lines, where the fluffy seeds float in the breeze created by passing trains and are distributed far and wide.

◀ Michaelmas daisies are the mainstay of many herbaceous borders in autumn. They put on a stunning display that often starts in September and lasts well into November.

Meadow saffron

Despite its resemblance to spring and autumn-flowering crocuses, meadow saffron is an unrelated plant that flowers in late summer and autumn. Pink flowers sprout from leafless bulbs in August and September, giving the garden some colour in this otherwise sparse season. All parts of the plant are poisonous, and it should not be confused with true saffron, which is used to colour and flavour food.

Wild meadow saffron grows in moist soils such as those of low-lying meadows and, in the Cotswolds especially, damp woods. Land drainage has reduced its spread, but it can still be seen growing wild on some sites in northern Dorset, Oxfordshire and south-eastern Wales.

► In the garden, meadow saffron is best grown in a lawn, preferably on a partially shaded site where the soil is damp. Avoid cutting the grass near the plant from August onwards.

Soapwort

If they are rubbed between forefinger and thumb, the leaves of soapwort create a slight but distinctly slippery froth, which can be used as a mild detergent. It has a gentler action than soap, and until quite recently it was regularly used to clean old, fragile fabrics of historic interest, such as ancient tapestries.

Soapwort is a member of the pink family. It was introduced to Britain from the Middle East, and cultivated as part of the cloth industry. It has become naturalised on roadsides, waste areas and damp woods in south-western England and northern Wales. The long-stalked flowers appear between July and late September, although the flowering season can be extended by regular deadheading.

◄ The pink flowers of soapwort make a fine show in late summer and early autumn. Many modern cultivated varieties produce extremely dense heads, including a double-flowered form.

Devil's-bit scabious

In the wild, devil's-bit scabious grows in a wide variety of habitats and soil types, so it is suitable for planting in most gardens. The first flowers appear in June, but careful, regular deadheading will persuade the plant to bear its dark purplish blue flowers well into October. The flowers produce a lot of nectar, making them popular with bees and late butterflies, such as the red admiral. Earlier in the year, the leaves provide food for caterpillars of the marsh fritillary butterfly. The plant gets its curious name from the truncated form of its rootstock, which was supposedly bitten off by the devil.

◄ Devil's-bit scabious is a member of the teasel family. It looks best if grown in a section of the garden that has been set aside as a miniature wild-flower meadow.

WILDLIFE WATCH

How can I grow autumn wild flowers?

● Goldenrods, Michaelmas daisies and soapwort are all easy to grow in the garden. However, to ensure prolific flowering from one year to the next, the plants should be divided every few years in spring. Each plant should be lifted and the young, outermost shoots carefully removed and replanted. The remains of the rootstock can then be discarded, because this older part of the plant rarely produces good displays of flowers. Dividing plants also avoids overcrowding, which generally leads to an increased risk of disease. Michaelmas daisies are particularly susceptible to powdery mildew, and are best divided each year in spring when the new shoots begin to emerge.

● Never take plants from the wild for your garden. Always buy native plants from reputable plant stockists.

Wild garden fruits

Many cultivated fruits have native ancestors that still thrive in woods and hedgerows. They can be surprisingly sweet and juicy, and are well worth encouraging if they by chance stray into a garden.

Currants

Both blackcurrants and redcurrants are deciduous shrubs that grow up to 2m (6ft 6in) tall in damp woodlands throughout Britain. In the wild, they flower during April and May, but cultivated forms have been bred to blossom later to avoid late spring frost damage to the blooms. They fruit in summer, and although the crops of wild plants are not as heavy as those of garden cultivars, they can be plentiful, providing food for birds and small mammals. Blackcurrants have a sweeter flavour than redcurrants, which taste slightly bitter unless well sweetened, and are best reserved for use in tarts and jams.

The two species are very similar, but have several differences, the most obvious being the colour and size of their fruits. The berries of redcurrants are smaller than those of blackcurrants, and have a luscious look. Redcurrant leaves are unscented and usually hairless, or almost so, whereas those of the blackcurrant are strong smelling and sticky beneath.

▶ The dark, glossy fruits of blackcurrant ripen in midsummer. The plant's leaves contain glands that give off a pungent, characteristic scent when bruised.

▶ Redcurrant berries form in tight, juicy-looking clusters which, unless protected by netting, are quickly stripped by fruit-eating birds, such as thrushes.

Apples

The wild apple native to Britain is the crab apple, which grows mainly in oak woods. The fruit is small – rarely more than 25mm (1in) across – and is sour and unpalatable to humans unless made into jelly or wine. The tree has stubby thorns, a feature that is not present in other apple trees. It also has smaller flowers, and the leaves are hairless, whereas those of cultivated species are often slightly downy.

In the wild, crab apple trees are scarce, outnumbered by those known as 'wildings'. These are trees that have sprouted from the discarded cores of cultivated apples. They are never like their parents, and every tree bears fruit with its own form and flavour.

▲ Wild apples are edible straight from the tree but examine them carefully before taking a bite. They are often attacked by wasps and other insects and, although the damage may be obvious, it is sometimes less so.

Gooseberries

In Victorian times, gooseberry competitions were common throughout Britain, with the first prize going to the heaviest berry of the day. These cultivated varieties could be the size of bantam eggs, and weigh 60g (2oz) – huge when compared to the fruits of their wild cousins, which never grow much bigger than 8g (¼oz).

Wild gooseberries grow in damp woodland, scrub and hedges. They are identified by their downy, three to five-lobed leaves, each sprouting above three sharp spines. The fruits are green or greenish yellow when ripe, with bristly hairs.

▲ In the wild, gooseberries seldom grow to more than 12mm (½in) long, and have a sharp, dry flavour. The remains of the flower often persist for a long time while the fruit is ripening.

Strawberries

The tiny fruits of wild strawberry have an intense flavour that cannot be matched by domestic varieties bred for size rather than taste. The wild strawberry is extremely common in woodland and scrub throughout Britain, partly because of the efficiency with which it spreads. After fruiting, the plant sends out horizontal stems – known as runners – with tiny rootless plantlets attached. When a plantlet makes contact with the soil, it starts to grow roots and develops into a new plant, genetically identical to its parent. If wild strawberries are grown in the garden, their runners should be removed, or the plants will soon take over.

▲ The wild strawberry's flowers have five white, unnotched petals. The bright red fruits appear throughout the spring and early summer along the edges of woodland rides and lanes. Some cultivated forms continue fruiting into autumn.

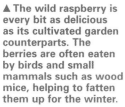

▲ The wild raspberry is every bit as delicious as its cultivated garden counterparts. The berries are often eaten by birds and small mammals such as wood mice, helping to fatten them up for the winter.

▼ Wild cherry fruits can be red, black or yellow, ripening on the tree from July onwards. Although not so sweet as cultivated varieties, they were often used in old country recipes, such as cherry pie.

Raspberries

The raspberry, which is related to the bramble, or blackberry, can be seen growing naturally in damp woodland and scrub, and on heaths, throughout Britain. Its erect, prickly stems or 'canes' bear compound leaves with up to seven leaflets, and flowers that open from May to August. The berries appear in late summer, and plants on sheltered sites may fruit until October.

The most common garden cultivars are the summer-fruiting type, which bear fruit on canes produced during the previous year's growth. These canes are best pruned to soil level after the berries have been picked.

FALSE FRUIT

Many of the structures that most people recognise as fruits are actually 'false fruits' to a botanist. A true fruit is formed from the ovary of the flower, as with the currant or gooseberry. The flesh of apples, strawberries, raspberries and cherries is formed in other ways.

In an apple, the ovary forms the core that contains the seeds or pips. The remainder of the apple is made from the receptacle – the area on which all the flower parts sit – which swells and envelops the ovary after pollination. In a strawberry, it is not the juicy flesh of the berry that is the true fruit, but the hard green specks that occur on the outside. Each one of these contains a seed. Raspberries are known as 'aggregate fruits'. Each fleshy sphere in the cluster that makes up the raspberry is an individual true fruit containing a seed, which is joined to its neighbours. The fruit of cherries has a stone with an inner wall surrounding a single seed.

Cherries

In its natural state, the wild cherry, or 'gean', is a woodland tree, related to the blackthorn and crab apple. It grows mainly on chalky soils in southern Britain. Dazzling white blossom – which opens before the leaves in spring – attractive peeling bark, autumn foliage colour and excellent timber make it one of the most popular native trees, regardless of its fruit.

Wild cherry fruits are smaller than those of cultivated varieties, with less flesh around the hard central stone. They can be bitter, but are often quite edible when ripe. Birds devour them in great quantities, and by carrying the stones away they help to spread the seed. As a result, wild cherries are quite likely to spring up in gardens without being deliberately planted.

Preparing for hibernation

As summer gives way to autumn, many animals start getting ready to face the winter. Having fortified themselves by eating as much as possible, they creep into burrows and crevices to sleep through the worst of the cold weather.

Towards the end of summer, as the trees and bushes become laden with fruit and nuts, many animals start feeding intensively in order to build up their reserves of energy. They know, instinctively, that hard times are ahead, and as summer turns to autumn they work hard to prepare for the winter. Some will stay active throughout the cold months, and simply need the extra energy to keep them warm. Others – mainly birds – escape the harsh weather by migrating to warmer regions, and need the energy to fuel their journeys. Still others get through the winter by slipping into a state of dormancy and if they fail to eat enough beforehand, they may starve in their sleep.

Nut harvest

Fruiting plants provide an energy-rich harvest for many of these animals. The edible dormouse, for example, relies on finding plenty of fruits, seeds and nuts to build up its fat reserves in autumn. It is a relatively recent addition to British wildlife, having been introduced to the Chilterns in 1902. It is still restricted to the Chiltern woodlands, but often ventures into mature gardens to feast on the fruits of garden plants. It may double its body weight by October, when it curls up in a sheltered site to spend the winter in a deep sleep. Its body processes slow right down to conserve energy, and by the time it emerges in April it will have lost all the weight it put on in autumn.

Foraging bats

A major reason for hibernation is that food is hard to find in winter. Bats are specialised hunters of aerial insects, which are very scarce in the cold months, so like the dormouse they eat as much as possible in autumn.

Three species – two pipistrelles and the long-eared bat – often overwinter in the roofs of houses and outbuildings, and may hunt intensively in gardens throughout September and October. They can

The edible dormouse is also known as the fat dormouse because it accumulates an impressive layer of fat during its short period of summer and early autumn activity. This will see it through seven or more months of hibernation.

be seen flitting through the gathering dusk, pipistrelles seizing tiny flies in mid-air while long-eared bats also glean small insects from the foliage of trees and shrubs.

Vanishing insects

Bats are forced to hibernate because their insect prey dwindles. Many adult insects simply die off in the cold weather, but some species creep into crevices, cool down and lie dormant. These include the many British species of ladybirds, some of which can be found in clusters in the garden. In common with other animals, they feed as well as they can in autumn before seeking out suitable

◄ Sensitive to the slightest sound signal that might betray insect prey, the long-eared bat's huge ears enable it to feed well in readiness for hibernation.

▼ Although they may jostle for position, these 11-spot ladybirds are likely to remain huddled in more or less the same position throughout the entire winter.

▶ These eyed hawk-moth pupae are encased in a tough 'skin' that helps protect them from the cold. They spend autumn and winter buried in the soil, and emerge in June.

▼ A hedgehog has the ideal body shape for hibernation. It spends the winter curled up in a tight ball among leaves and vegetation, its shape helping to minimise heat loss.

places in which to see out the cold weather. Winter sites used by ladybirds range from below the soil to high in the foliage of pine trees. The 11-spot ladybird, for example, favours the dead foliage of plants such as thistles and teasels, or hides among dry plant stems, so it is important to avoid over-tidying the garden in autumn.

Hidden hedgehogs
The hedgehog is another animal that hibernates because the small animals that it eats are hard to find in winter. It builds up a thick layer of fat in autumn by feeding heavily on slugs, snails, worms and beetles, then curls up in a nest that it makes among fallen branches and piles of leaves. Garden bonfire heaps often tempt hedgehogs, and since they are often asleep by early November in cold years, it is essential to check any garden rubbish heaps built for lighting on Bonfire Night.

Adult hedgehogs usually survive the winter without too many problems, but young animals born late in the previous summer may not have time to build up the weight of body fat needed for them to survive. A good food supply is vital for these animals, and it helps if gardeners avoid using pesticides that destroy their prey – and possibly poison the hedgehogs themselves.

Cold comfort
The animals that are eaten by hedgehogs are also the main prey of frogs, toads and newts. These amphibians have no way of controlling their body temperature, so as the days and nights get colder in autumn, they start to cool down and become inactive. This makes hunting difficult – especially as prey becomes harder to find – and also makes them vulnerable to attack. So in late autumn, with their body temperature much reduced, they enter a state of torpor very like hibernation.

To be safe, they must find appropriate places to spend the winter. Small abandoned mammal burrows and other holes in the ground are favoured, as well as sheds and crevices under paving slabs. Gardeners can help by providing suitable sites, such as piles of stacked branches.

Many of the slugs and snails that these animals eat also hibernate. Garden snails seek refuge in the crannies in stone walls and the sides of wooden compost bins, and under timber stacked on the ground. They choose places that will give them protection not only from the cold weather, but from predators such as birds and shrews, which would make short work of such helpless prey.

Dormant phase
Rather than overwinter as adult insects, some British moths contrive to pass the cold season as pupae. The pupal stage is a comparatively inactive phase of a moth's life cycle, when it needs no food and is well protected by a hardened, shiny brown 'skin'. This is much less vulnerable to frost damage than either a soft-bodied caterpillar or an adult moth. However, moth pupae make ideal prey for hungry predators and have no real means of defence, so the caterpillars make their way into safe retreats, often underground, before metamorphosing into pupae.

Several common garden butterflies, such as commas, peacocks and brimstones, hibernate as adults. Small tortoiseshells do the same, and

often move into sheds and houses in autumn in search of suitable sites. By the end of October they will have settled, but any that try to overwinter in houses are often too warm, so they become active too early, run out of energy and die before spring.

▲ Suitable crevices and retreats for garden snails are often in short supply, so good spots can become crammed full of snails in late autumn. On mild nights they sometimes venture out to feed, even in winter.

▼ By the time they seek out their winter refuges in the autumn, common frogs are normally plump and well fed. They need these energy reserves if they are to survive the winter months with no food.

Garden hedges

Rambling country hedgerows provide vital food and shelter for wildlife. On a smaller scale, a garden hedge of native plants can be just as valuable, and far more interesting than a string of exotic conifers.

Many garden hedges consist of shrubs that have been introduced to Britain from other parts of the world. These may make excellent hedges, but their alien foliage supports very few native insects and other small animals when compared to native plants. Some gardeners might see this as an advantage, because it makes the hedge less vulnerable to damage, but it also makes the garden less welcoming to wildlife of all kinds. Flourishing insect populations attract other animals such as insectivorous birds, and are interesting and often colourful in their own right. The beauty of native plants is often underrated, although most people admire them when they grow in semi-wild hedgerows. Yet there is no reason why a garden hedge cannot be planted with the same species, and act as a magnet to passing wildlife.

Mixed planting

Garden hedges usually consist of just one type of plant, but a collection of different plants attracts more wildlife and often looks more colourful. The hedge could include hawthorn, spindle, maple and hornbeam, as well as various types of native wild rose.

Dog rose, for example, has a carefree, rambling pattern of growth that can make it difficult to manage in a hedge by itself, so it is best planted with other species. Its arching stems will produce an abundance of pinkish white flowers in summer, attracting many nectar-feeding insects to the garden.

Hornbeam makes a handsome hedge, with a striking resemblance to beech. In autumn its bright green leaves change to pale gold or vibrant orange.

BERRY-BEARING HEDGES

Any native hedging plants provide shelter and nesting sites for animals. Species that produce crops of edible berries attract even more creatures.

Hawthorn is one of the most common hedging plants on farms, because its thorny growth makes an excellent stockproof barrier. It is also an excellent choice for the garden. Its dense crown is popular with nesting birds, especially finches. In autumn and winter its clusters of glossy red berries attract birds, such as blackbirds and thrushes, as well as small mammals, including mice, voles and squirrels. In early spring, the fragrant white flowers are a source of nectar for many insects.

The sharp thorns of blackthorn make an even more impenetrable hedge, and in autumn the plant – a species of wild plum – bears the blue-black sloes that are eagerly sought out by robins, thrushes and other birds during the colder months. Its white flowers open while the leaves are still in bud, bringing early colour to the garden in spring, and some birds may nest among its protective thorny

branches. However, wounds caused by the thorns may become infected, so it should be treated with caution.

Spindle adds superb autumn colour to the garden, its leaves erupting into a dazzling display of vibrant reds. Its coral-pink fruits split open to reveal bright orange seeds that attract birds such as robins. Blackberry also provides juicy berries for small birds and mammals in autumn, as well as nectar earlier in the year. It is a sprawling, prickly plant, so it needs careful siting and management to stop it taking over the garden.

▲ The vivid autumn colour of spindle is matched by the delicate, sculptural beauty of its fruits. The plant can act as a winter host for the black bean aphid, so avoid growing it near the vegetable patch.

◄ When the red fruits – or haws – of hawthorn ripen in autumn, they may be targeted by flocks of waxwings driven south from their Scandinavian or Russian breeding grounds by food shortages.

◄ Succulent fruits of the blackberry or bramble are popular with both humans and wildlife, but the plant needs plenty of space. In summer the white or pink flowers will attract many butterflies and moths.

▲ A hedge of mixed species, such as hawthorn and blackthorn, will provide an autumn feast for garden wildlife. Sloes and haws attract many birds, including thrushes, finches, robins and pigeons.

◄ Perhaps surprisingly, fruit is a favourite food of foxes. Blackberries, rose hips, apples, pears and plums are all eaten with relish. The sugary juices taste good, and they are a useful source of energy.

NATIVE TREES FOR THE HEDGEROW

Several native trees make excellent hedging plants, with careful trimming. They include the yew, which is the only native conifer that is commonly used to form a hedge. Although slow-growing at first, it eventually develops into a solid, hardy, evergreen hedge that needs minimal trimming, and can be clipped into wonderfully ornamental shapes. The foliage and seeds are poisonous, but the bright red, berry-like fruits are extremely popular with birds and some mammals.

Beech becomes a tall, spreading tree when left to grow, but it can also be trimmed into a compact, easily managed hedge. It offers a kaleidoscope of colours that mirror the seasons. During autumn and winter the dead foliage is a deep russet brown. In spring this is replaced by bright green leaves, which turn a rich, deep green in summer. Purple and copper-leaved varieties can be planted for more colour.

In the wild, beech prefers free-draining soils over limestone or sand, a factor that should be considered when choosing hedging plants. If the soil is heavy clay, then beech is best avoided. Hornbeam is the perfect alternative for such heavy soils, since it has many of the same qualities as beech. It is an excellent choice for the garden because it is easily clipped, becoming very dense and retaining some of its dead leaves in winter.

Field maple also makes a lovely hedge, especially in autumn when its wide five-lobed leaves turn a dramatic bright yellow. It can be trimmed into a neat, effective hedge and may even be used for topiary.

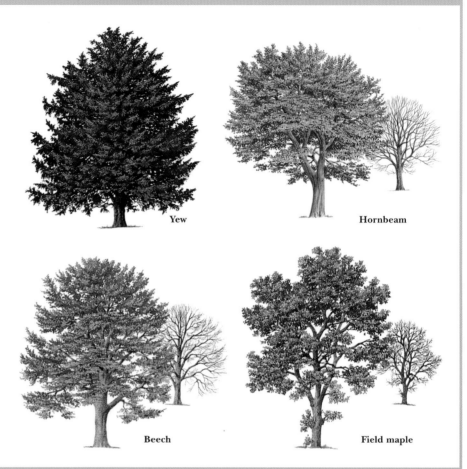

Yew   Hornbeam

Beech   Field maple

▶ The elongated hips of dog rose appear in August after the flowers have fallen, and often persist through the autumn and well into winter if they are not devoured by birds.

▼ Field rose hips are shorter and often rounder than those of the dog rose. Rose hips contain a lot of vitamin C and are popular with many small mammals, such as grey squirrels.

In autumn the scarlet fruits, or hips, of the dog rose provide welcome food for garden birds, such as thrushes.

Native dogwood grows well in a mixed hedge. Although it is inconspicuous for much of the year, it comes into its own in autumn when its leaves turn wine-red and it produces black pea-sized berries that attract hungry birds. The young stems are dark red, providing a wonderful display in winter. Hard pruning in spring encourages young growth, but since this makes the hedge look gappy it is often better to clip it into shape, in the same way as other hedging plants.

Evergreen hedges

Britain's temperate climate is not ideal for evergreen plants, so there are not many native species. However, some do occur and, as well as yew, both holly and box grow into superb hedges – although they may take a long time to reach a suitable size.

▲ Holly berries are a favourite food of the blackbird. Other thrushes, wood pigeons and starlings also eat them and the female plants are often stripped of their fruit before they can be cut for Christmas decorations.

▲ The round, bitter black berries of dogwood grow in clusters, which ripen in August and September. The seeds are distributed by birds in their droppings.

Holly fares well in shady gardens and can tolerate conditions that may be too harsh for other trees. It can be clipped and shaped to form a prickly barrier that will deter trespassers and keep animals out or in. The berries attract birds in autumn and winter, but only female holly plants bear berries.

Box is a valuable hedging plant for formal gardens, because it can be clipped into architectural forms that keep their shape. Well-grown plants are expensive, however, and require several years to reach any great height. The leaves give off a 'tom-cat' smell when brushed. A good alternative is wild native privet, which is quick and easy to grow.

▼ Native wild privet produces black berries that are eaten by birds, including bullfinches. It is a better choice for a wildlife hedge than Japanese privet, which rarely flowers.

Wild privet was popular as a hedging plant in Elizabethan gardens, although it did have a tendency to shed its leaves in harsh winters. It was generally superseded by the oval-leaved, semi-evergreen Japanese or garden privet, but this non-native plant is far less valuable to wildlife.

Wild privet produces sprays of sweetly scented, ivory-white flowers above glossy, elongated leaves during early summer, followed by shiny black berries in autumn. These berries are poisonous to humans, but are much relished by various garden birds and the occasional flock of winter-visiting waxwings.

▲ The dark green upper surfaces of the yew's needle-like foliage contrast with the paler undersides. As with other hedging plants, the red berries attract garden birds.

The leaves are also the main food of the spectacular privet hawk-moth.

Needle-leaved conifers make excellent plants for single-species hedges, their evergreen foliage providing a verdant backdrop for borders all year round. All the conifer species commonly used for hedges are exotics apart from the yew, which is arguably one of the finest of all hedging plants. It is slow-growing, like box, but this in itself is useful once the hedge is established.

WILDLIFE WATCH

When and how should I plant a garden hedge?

● A hedge can be planted at virtually any time of year, but the best season is autumn. At this time the plants are able to send their roots into warm soil and can begin to establish themselves before the cold winter weather arrives, but they are not at risk of drying out.

● Good ground preparation is essential to get a hedge off to a good start. Mark out where it is to go, then dig a trench along its length and place the topsoil to one side. Ideally, the trench should be at least half a metre (20in) wide.

● Break up the subsoil with a fork and incorporate well-rotted compost or manure. Replace the topsoil and leave the ground to settle for a few weeks.

● Choose bare-rooted plants for autumn planting, that is plants that have been grown in fields, then dug up and bundled together. These are often less expensive than plants grown in containers, and their roots take better than those of plants that have been confined in pots.

● Place the plants at least 30cm (12in) apart, planting them at the same depth as they were originally grown. A soil mark on the lower part of each stem indicates this. Mix a couple of handfuls of bonemeal with the soil used to backfill each hole.

● Keep the plants well watered during their first summer, and trim off half their height every winter for the first three years, to make them bush out.

Wildlife in puddles and pools

A muddy puddle on a parkland track can attract all kinds of thirsty animals. Some of the deeper pools even harbour tiny creatures that are specially adapted to live in them.

The shallow water of a wheel-rut or puddle and the surrounding mud form one of the smallest and most unstable of all habitats, yet such ephemeral pools support a good number of plants and animals. Whether they are sheltered by spreading tree foliage or exposed in open grassland, pools and puddles become more common in the cooler, wetter autumn months. They provide drinking and bathing water for all kinds of visitors, and some are inhabited by unusual, and even rare, creatures.

Short-lived puddles and pools have been forming for millions of years in such hollows as the cavities left by uprooted trees, or the footprints of big grazing animals. They provide safe refuges for small animals, free from the competitive pressures of more established environments, and over time various creatures have evolved ways of making the most of these opportunities. Each animal has its own particular requirements, and since every pool and puddle is subtly different, each one supports its own unique wildlife.

Drinking water

Many of the ruts and puddles found on parkland are the result of human activity, but some are created or enlarged by animals. Either way, an upwelling of clear, running

In autumn, puddles are commonplace in shady wooded areas. They often form along bridleways or tracks used by park vehicles.

RARE PLANTS

The disturbed margins of puddles can be ideal sites for several rare plants, such as the aptly named mudwort. A rapid annual life cycle enables this species to make the most of such short-lived habitats, yet its occurrence is fitful. It can reappear after years of absence.

In some regions, the pale pink flowers of the increasingly rare grass-poly – a relative of the more familiar purple loosestrife – can be found growing in wet hollows. The waterlogged fringes of puddles may also support the woolly leaved marsh cudweed.

Mudwort is confined to drying mud at the edges of pools or puddles, mainly in the Midlands. Its dainty pink or white flowers appear from June to October.

Mudwort
Limosella aquatica

water or a shallow puddle can be a magnet for local wildlife. Fresh water will tempt a variety of birds down from the safety of the treetops. On quiet woodland rides and tracks, for example, a clear pool in an undisturbed rut can provide a rare glimpse of a hawfinch or crossbill as it pauses to drink or bathe.

Many puddles contain more than just water, however. They often have concentrations of mineral salts, and these attract animals that are suffering from mineral deficiency in their diets. These may range from treetop butterflies to deer and even wild park cattle.

When such 'salt-licks' or sources of drinking water are regularly visited by large animals, the surrounding ground soon becomes churned up into soft mud. With every footstep the mud gets deeper and deeper, and in low-lying areas it may never dry out. As more animals visit to drink, more mud and soil is removed on their coats. In time, this slow process of accidental excavation can enlarge a small puddle into a big one, and may eventually result in a sizeable pool.

Virgin territory
Every new puddle is open to rapid colonisation by species that cannot cope with intense rivalry for food and water, or cannot defend themselves from the predators that live in more permanent ponds.

With no competition or enemies to keep them in check, populations can boom, but the bonanza of life may be short-lived. The temporary nature of small pools means that the animals must be highly mobile or have short life cycles if they are to thrive.

Insects that spend their first few weeks as aquatic larvae are particularly well adapted to life in temporary pools. A muddy puddle can provide a perfect nursery for midges, for example. From spring onwards, swarms of male midges can often be seen dancing above the water surface in an effort to attract females, which will lay their eggs in the water after mating with the males.

Breathing tubes
The pools often contain a lot of the organic and mineral nutrients that support plant life, and this can encourage a 'bloom' of algae and bacteria that ultimately uses up most of the oxygen in the water. These provide aquatic animals with plenty to eat, however, so those that can find another oxygen supply often flourish in large numbers. In the shallow margins, rat-tailed maggots – the aquatic larvae of some species of hoverfly – feed on the nutrient-rich detritus that is washed into the water. Gills are of little use for breathing in such silty, stagnant waters, and the rat-tailed maggot survives by breathing air through a tube at the end of its body, which it extends to the water surface like a snorkel.

Mosquito larvae use a similar system, and black, fluffy-looking clouds of the insects can often be seen hanging from their breathing tubes at the surface of the water. If they are disturbed, the larvae wriggle to the bottom of the pool, and lie low until the danger is likely to be past.

▲ A speckled wood butterfly may linger on the site of a dried-up puddle, probing the earth with its long tongue in search of crystallised salts.

Deeper, more long-lasting pools may contain animals that spend their entire lives under water. In some, swarms of tiny water fleas turn the surface waters pink as they multiply on a rich diet of microscopic algae. It is sometimes possible to pick out the minute, grey, torpedo-shaped form of another crustacean, *Cyclops*, as it darts between the bobbing water fleas in search of tiny aquatic invertebrates on which it feeds. Such pools also provide homes for pond skaters, where they are safe from submerged predators, such as fish and water boatmen. On large, well-established pools, swarms of these predatory bugs patrol the water surface for insects that have crash-landed and become ensnared by the surface tension. Deep pools formed beneath the upturned roots of fallen trees may provide more stable, sheltered microclimates, in which water beetles can live and breed.

Suspended animation
Some aquatic species have become so specialised for life in temporary pools that they are able to survive prolonged periods of dormancy if their puddles dry up. They survive as eggs or even as adults, sealing themselves into the

Crossbills spend much of their time feeding on conifer seeds high up in the tree tops. They must drink, though, and their visits to puddles may offer a chance for a closer view.

BATHING POOLS

Birds visit puddles for several reasons, including to drink, to collect mud for nest building and to bathe. Bathing is very important – accumulated dirt and grime clogging the feathers reduce their efficiency in flight, as insulation against the cold, and as protection from the rain. Also, since plumage plays an important role in courtship and display, tatty feathers may make winning a breeding partner much harder.

After a vigorous bath to rinse off dust, grease and parasites, a bird will retreat to a safe perch to smooth down its feathers and re-anoint them with oil from the preen gland. For small birds, which overheat easily, bathing is also a way of keeping cool in hot weather.

Some species, such as house sparrows, also bathe in dust. The fine sediment that collects at the bottom of a dried-up puddle is perfect for dust-bathing.

▲ Regular bathing enables this yellowhammer to maintain its plumage. It often uses pools that form where large animals have trampled the wet soil into mud.

▶ On warm days, small birds, such as this young blackbird, can suffer from the heat. A flurry of feathers in a parkland puddle can be a good way to cool down and clean up.

Puddle plants

The bright green foliage of water starworts may appear in the deeper, more long-lasting puddles. Shaded pools beneath trees in wooded parkland often seem to overflow with the pale green foliage of water pepper, while at the waterlogged edges of sunny woodland rides the lilac-coloured flowers of water mint and the deep reddish brown flowers of water figwort buzz with bees and wasps. In trampled mud, the round flower heads of pineapple weed, introduced from America in the 19th century, are increasingly seen.

dried mud for weeks or even months, and then reviving when heavy rain soaks the mud and recreates the puddles. Such downpours can stir up millions of miniature crustaceans called ostracods from deep within the dried mud and leaf mould. Their shrimp-like bodies are protected by two shells that clamp tightly together, rather like those of a cockle, to stop the animals drying out during their dormancy.

◀ The puddles that form in ruts are often deep enough to survive warm, sunny spells without drying out, making them valuable to wildlife in summer.

▲ In autumn, red deer stags wallow in muddy puddles after urinating in them. The pungent smell informs both females and rival males of their presence.

▲ Once sealed in their shells, tiny, seed-like ostracods are able to survive prolonged periods out of water. These crustaceans can lie dormant in the soil for several years.

▲ The eggs of fairy shrimps can remain in dry soil for months until rainfall revives them and they hatch into their delicate, swimming adult form.

▲ Exposed margins of muddy puddles may support the feathery foliage of pineapple weed – a pineapple-scented relative of the more colourful mayweeds.

Mud stirred up by heavy vehicles can bring dormant seeds to the surface, and spring sunshine can cause these dark patches of earth to erupt with the beautiful pinks and purples of common spotted and early purple orchids. Later, in autumn, any sodden area of park and woodland is liable to be colonised by fungi, pushing up through the wet soil and dead leaves.

New Forest pools
Boggy areas of the New Forest National Park are renowned for their diverse aquatic life. Local specialities include fairy shrimps, which hatch and lay eggs in the puddles formed after rain. When the puddles dry out, the adult fairy shrimps die, but their eggs survive in the dried mud.

Many pools on New Forest heathland dry up in summer. During autumn and winter the pools refill, but the water is acid and stained dark orange-brown by the peaty soils. This combination of features means that many of the plants that

grow in the temporary pools are characteristic of the New Forest, and rarely found elsewhere.

One such specialist is the small fleabane, which can be found growing among yellow centaury, pennyroyal and chaffweed near the pool edges. Hampshire purslane is another New Forest speciality that, within its limited confines, can become quite common. The New Forest is one of the last strongholds of coral necklace. Its trailing pink stems, stippled with clusters of white flowers, are easy to spot among the short turf of the pool margins.

Autumn brings a flush of colour to damp hollows in wooded parkland, as fungi such as this *Boletus versicolor* begin to appear in the damp leaf litter.

CLUES IN THE MUD

A muddy puddle margin can be the perfect place for discovering animal tracks. These may indicate the presence of shy or nocturnal mammals that are rarely seen by casual observers.

In country parks, the large prints of fallow and roe deer are a common sight, but the tiny ones left by the hooves of muntjac deer can prove more challenging to find.

Look carefully for the big footprints of badgers, with their broad pads and long claw marks, and the neat, diamond-shaped prints of foxes that may have stopped to drink at shallow pools. On soft ground even the feet of lightweight

weasels or stoats may leave an identifiable depression, giving an insight into the activities of these bold little hunters.

Closer to town, paths and tracks through parks and gardens tend to be littered with heavy, splayed dog prints or the rounded, clawless prints of cats. In some areas it may be possible to pick out the long-toed prints of hedgehogs, or even the tiny claw marks left by brown rats.

▲ The badger gains most of the moisture it needs from earthworms, but during dry periods it will seek out puddles after dusk.

▶ Soft mud at the edge of a puddle takes an excellent impression of any footprint. The heavy badger leaves broad, strongly clawed prints.

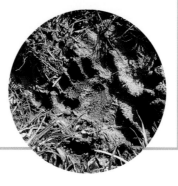

WILDLIFE WATCH

Where can I see puddle and pool wildlife?

● Undisturbed puddles in the larger, more rural parks attract a broad variety of aquatic and visiting life.

● Muddy puddles near gates are so disturbed that few aquatic creatures can live in them, but they do provide birds, such as house martins, with a good source of mud for their nests.

● Roadside puddles in parks provide opportunities to watch birds drinking and bathing – and a car makes a very effective hide.

Urban buildings – useful shelters

Office blocks, churches and other tall buildings situated close to town parks are valuable to wildlife. Owls, mice and beetles are among those that often take advantage of the quiet refuges they provide.

When leaves start to fall from the trees, the buildings that overlook town and city parks become increasingly visible through the thinning foliage. This may be a source of regret to people who visit the parks for a break from city life, but the buildings can be surprisingly important to the animals that feed among the trees, because they provide vital shelter and secure nesting sites. In fact, some animals might find it hard to survive in the park if the buildings were not there.

This is particularly true of some parkland birds. One of the most important factors when choosing a nesting site is height. The higher the nest, the more likely the birds' eggs and nestlings are to be safe from prowling predators, such as foxes, which are becoming increasingly common in built-up areas.

Kestrels, probably the most familiar birds of prey, are among several species that make use of buildings. In open country, kestrels can nest in tree cavities or disused crows' nests, but the birds that hunt in town parks find that ledges on tall buildings make excellent substitutes. One survey of kestrels in London found that the number of breeding pairs per square kilometre or mile was much the same as in open country.

Convenience food

The barn owls that hunt in larger, semi-rural parks are more likely to nest in nearby buildings than in the park itself. As their name suggests, they have been associated with farm buildings for centuries, but they also nest in bell towers and quiet churches, where they find plenty of prey among the dense vegetation of overgrown churchyards. They can find similar sites in and around large parks.

A ready source of food is vital when the breeding season begins in early spring. Owls cannot afford to waste time travelling long distances when there are hungry mouths to feed. The male is kept busy feeding the female while she incubates the eggs, and once the chicks have

The house mouse is common in all kinds of buildings, from old churches to modern factories. It can be an important source of food for urban owls.

A barn owl descends on silent wings to snatch up a victim from the long grass of a neglected churchyard. A steady supply of mice, rats and voles is vital to a successful breeding season.

DESTRUCTIVE BEETLES

To an insect, the timbers of an old building are just like the dead wood of a fallen tree. Some beetles use the wood as food for their young, and in the process they gradually reduce it to dust. The most notorious of these insects is the death-watch beetle. Adults attract mates by tapping their heads rhythmically against the timber. Their voracious larvae feed on damp wood, chewing out tunnels that weaken the timber and may make it

collapse. Death-watch beetles are responsible for the musty smell that pervades many churches.

Equally damaging is the smaller furniture beetle, the larvae of which are better known as woodworm. They attack softwood timbers, such as floorboards and roof beams, as well as furniture.

It may be less than 9mm (⅜in) long, but the death-watch beetle can cause serious damage to the timbers that support old buildings.

▲ A pipistrelle bat is able to squeeze its tiny body through amazingly small gaps of less than 10mm (⅜in) to gain access to a secure roost.

▶ In autumn, a butterfly from a late-hatching brood will often retreat to a sheltered building. Many such butterflies do not survive the winter, but some may emerge to breed.

hatched the demand for food is relentless. Despite this the hard-working parents can produce two broods of four to seven young each year.

The main signs that these secretive owls are about are usually regurgitated pellets, containing the indigestible remains of prey, found below the nest. Tawny owls produce similar pellets, and are much more common than barn owls in town parks. Strictly nocturnal, tawny owls usually roost and nest in trees, but they may take over cavities in nearby buildings. Their ghostly hoots and sharp '*ke-wick*' calls are often to be heard in the night around wooded parks and large churchyards.

Although now less numerous than the buzzard, the kestrel is the most conspicuous bird of prey in parks and built-up areas.

Bat colonies

In the warmer months, owls share the night sky with bats. Britain's smallest bats, the pipistrelles, are particularly common in parks, possibly because they favour buildings for roosting and breeding. They make little secret of their presence, often squeaking furiously before emerging to hunt at dusk.

Bats choose warm, sheltered places to breed in summer, because their young are vulnerable to cold. The warmer they are, the faster they grow, and the better their chances of survival. In late autumn, however, the bats move to cooler sites to hibernate, such as crevices beneath roof tiles. Such places

keep them dry, but allow their bodies to cool right down and use as little energy as possible over the winter. Butterflies, such as the small tortoiseshell and red admiral, employ the same strategy, and are often found hibernating in cool buildings near the parks and gardens where they foraged for nectar in summer.

WILDLIFE WATCH

Where can I see wildlife in urban buildings?

● Local wildlife trusts have information on sites that are known to have nesting birds or bat roosts.

● Spend some time watching to see which (if any) buildings are favoured by kestrels as roosting and nesting sites.

● Listening for calls, such as the begging calls of baby birds and the high-pitched squeaks of bats and mice, can help pinpoint sites. Then try visiting at dawn or dusk to watch for wildlife activity. At sundown, for instance, owls and bats leave to hunt.

Autumn retreats

A snug winter sanctuary is vital for many parkland creatures, from bats and frogs to mice and bees. The provision of a wooden box or some other simple weatherproof shelter greatly improves their chances of survival.

Every year animals that live in urban parks find it harder to find cosy places in which to spend the winter. Dead timber and wild corners, where they can build nests and hideaways, are often removed or tidied up in the interests of safety or neatness. One solution is for park staff to be less zealous in autumn. Another is for them to install specially designed homes along the lines of nestboxes that are put up for birds.

Bat and hedgehog boxes

A bat box is very like a bird nestbox, but it has a slot at the back of the floor that allows bats to climb in from below. Bats are very choosy about their roosting sites, and although bat boxes are often successful, the reasons why some boxes are favoured while others remain empty are not clear. Many park authorities put up bat boxes and several may be sited in the same area in the hope that the local bats will find some suitable for roosting by day and, possibly, hibernating in winter. Tall trees in nearby gardens could also be used for bat boxes.

◄ Bat boxes can be sited in clusters on the trunk of a tall tree. They must be shaded and, preferably, should face out into a ride or clearing so the bats have a clear flight path in and out of each box.

▼ Ready-made hedgehog homes such as this one are available, but they can also be built from timber. The box should be situated in a quiet corner where the hedgehog can approach under cover and will not be disturbed in winter.

A hedgehog box is just as easy to make, and provided it is well insulated, dry and airy, hedgehogs may choose it as a hibernation site in autumn. Such boxes are safer than many other sites, such as the snug piles of timber that turn out to be bonfire heaps.

Frogs and toads

Although all amphibians breed in ponds and pools, they spend a lot of time hunting on land. They need

sheltered places where they can hide from the sun and wind, which dry out their delicate skins. Frogs, toads and newts will take refuge in nooks and crannies in rock gardens, specially constructed stacks of rock, rubble or timber, or beneath paving slabs or sheets of corrugated iron. They will also use these refuges for hibernating, so it is important that they are in place by autumn.

◄ A few carefully placed roof-tiles or broken flowerpots provide welcome retreats for toads and other amphibians that need to shelter from the sun during the day.

Mouse house

Dormice are famous for their long winter sleep, and safe hibernation sites are vital to their survival. Hazel dormice in particular have become scarce, and every effort should be made to protect them.

Conservation efforts are under way and park keepers responsible for wooded areas with resident dormice often help by providing them with specially designed nestboxes. These resemble those used by small birds, such as tits, but they have entrance holes on the side or back of the box so they are more easily accessible from the tree trunk.

Insect refuges

Most of the larger animals that live in parks and gardens rely on smaller creatures to provide them with food. Without insects and other small animals, the whole food chain would collapse. Many insects have been badly hit by the widespread use of pesticides, but helping them to survive the winter by providing suitable refuges in autumn can do a lot to restore populations.

Many small insects naturally crawl into such cavities as the hollow stems of dead plants. The plants can be bundled together in lengths of clay drainpipe to make very effective winter retreats. Bunched drinking straws or rolled-up corrugated cardboard can be used as substitutes. A more durable alternative can be made by drilling holes in a block of wood. The holes should be 7–10mm (¼–⅜in) in diameter, and up to 20mm (⅜in) deep.

Vital pollinators

These refuges will attract lacewings – which control damaging aphids – and solitary bees, including the common mason, rose leaf-cutter and wool carder bees. Insects such as these bees are vital to flowering plants that need pollinating to produce their fruits and seeds. The berries that make shrubs such as pyracantha and cotoneaster so attractive in autumn would not appear if there were no insects to pollinate the flowers.

Bumblebees are important pollinators, and they can be encouraged by providing bumblebee boxes. These can be made above or below ground, but should be protected from mice by 10mm (⅜in) wire mesh both at the entrance and, if it is not enclosed, at the bottom of the nest chamber. Some nesting material such as dry wood shavings will encourage the bees to move in.

▲ Britain's smallest mouse, the harvest mouse, normally builds a round nest out of straw, but a tennis ball with a hole cut in it makes an acceptable substitute.

◄ An edible dormouse's chances of surviving the winter are improved by provision of a nestbox. These boxes make regular surveys to monitor dormouse activity much easier.

▼ Green lacewings, such as this common species, are active well into autumn but need a warm nook in which to sleep during the cold winter months.

▶ Bumblebees and carder bees will often nest in specially made boxes or abandoned birdboxes. Queen bees may also use them for their winter hibernation.

WILDLIFE WATCH

Where can I find more information?

● Bat Conservation Trust, Unit 2, 15 Cloisters House, 8 Battersea Park Road, London SW8 4BG (telephone 020 7627 2629) or visit www.bats.org.uk

● British Hedgehog Preservation Society, Hedgehog House, Dhustone, Ludlow, SY8 3PL (telephone 01584 890 801) or visit www.britishhedgehogs.org.uk

● Mammal Society, 2B Inworth Street, London SW11 3EP (telephone 020 7350 2200) or visit www.abdn.ac.uk/mammal

● Froglife, White Lodge, London Road, Peterborough PE7 0LG (telephone 01733 558 444) or visit www.froglife.org

● Buglife – the Invertebrate Conservation Trust, 170A Park Road, Peterborough PE1 2UF (telephone 01733 201 210) or visit www.buglife.org.uk

● Henry Doubleday Research Association, Ryton Organic Gardens, Coventry CV8 3LG (telephone 024 7630 3517) or visit www.gardenorganic.org.uk

Autumn park activity

As temperatures fall and morning mists start to shroud lakes and ponds, parkland animals prepare for the coming winter by stocking up on food, or seeking out safe refuges where they can hide away until spring.

Redwings and fieldfares

The bright berries that appear on parkland shrubs in autumn often attract migrant fieldfares and redwings. These thrushes arrive between September and November, having flown south from Scandinavia to escape the northern cold. They tend to travel by night and feed by day, and the thin, squeaky contact calls of redwing flocks can sometimes be heard as they pass over towns. Fieldfares are bigger and noisier than redwings, flying off with loud 'chacking' calls when disturbed, and perching conspicuously in the tops of trees and shrubs. The two species often feed together, especially on hawthorn, but may raid any fruiting shrubs and trees that they can find.

◀ **A redwing looks like a small song thrush, but has reddish flanks and bold pale eyebrows. It feeds on the ground as well as in berry-bearing trees and bushes.**

◀ **Fieldfares are gregarious birds that usually travel and feed in flocks. They are the most striking of the thrushes, with strongly contrasted plumage.**

Great spotted woodpecker

An erratic tapping in park woodland can often be traced to a great spotted woodpecker, usually halfway up a tree, hacking into damaged timber in search of juicy insect grubs. The sound is quite unlike the loud, rapid drumming that the bird uses as a territorial call in spring. Both sexes have bright red undertails that show up well when they are feeding in the branches, as do their large white shoulder patches, especially when many of the leaves have fallen. As great spotted woodpeckers move through the park, they fly from tree to tree in a series of distinctive swoops.

▲ **The distinctive great spotted woodpecker is often easy to watch as it forages for prey.**

◄ A familiar bird in parks and gardens, the chaffinch has a thick, pointed bill that is ideal for cracking tough seeds. This one is a male.

◄ Like chaffinches, but with darker heads, bramblings may turn up in large numbers when food is hard to find in northern Europe.

Chaffinches and bramblings

At the end of the nesting season, breeding pairs of finches abandon their territories and search for food in large nomadic flocks, often of several species. Chaffinches, for example, often feed alongside the very similar but much less common bramblings, which fly in from northern Europe in autumn. At this time they feed mainly on seeds, on the ground, and in urban parks they gather beneath birdfeeders to pick up the seed scattered by more acrobatic tits and nuthatches. In open areas the flocks often go unnoticed as they forage quietly among the grass, until they burst into the air in a flurry of white wingbars.

Sparrowhawk

Flocks of small birds that feed in parkland in autumn make tempting prey for the sparrowhawk – a specialised ambush hunter that has become increasingly common in urban parks and gardens. It is not as easy to see as the hovering, sharp-winged kestrel, because it usually stays out of sight until it is ready to strike. Then there is a sudden commotion as the hawk dives over a hedge in hot pursuit of a chaffinch, or maybe a redwing, and careers off through the trees – offering no more than a glimpse of barred plumage and an angry yellow eye.

► Shortish, broad wings and a long tail give the sparrowhawk great agility in the air, which is vital when hunting among trees.

Great crested grebe

Large park lakes can act as winter refuges for many waterbirds, from coots and ducks to geese, swans and even cormorants. The most elegant of these lake dwellers are the great crested grebes, which gather in large numbers on broad open waters in autumn. Although they soon lose their spectacular breeding plumage they are still eye-catching, with long, gleaming white necks, and long dagger bills that they use to catch fish while diving underwater. These birds are now quite common, probably numbering around 16,000 in autumn and winter, including young birds and some migrants from the Continent.

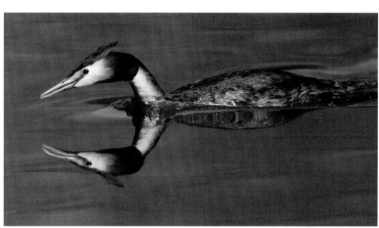

◄ Still resplendent in summer plumage in early autumn, this great crested grebe will moult its long crest and dark cheek tufts as the days grow shorter.

Common toad

From about mid-October, common toads start to look for secure refuges where they can spend the winter. They favour cool, fairly dry sites in holes beneath rocks or logs, which insulate them from the frost. They may hibernate alone, but if the site is particularly good, it may be used by several toads at once, and occasionally other animals, such as newts and lizards. If the toads have fed well in autumn they can survive the winter without eating at all, because their cool bodies use so little energy.

► Watching intently, this toad is alert to any flicker of movement that might betray a potential meal. It must eat well to prepare for hibernation.

The long-eared bat will eventually run out of insect prey as autumn advances, and be forced into hibernation.

Long-eared bat

Several species of bat hunt in parks well into autumn, building up their energy reserves in preparation for their winter hibernation. The long-eared bat specialises in hunting among trees and bushes, since the super-sensitive hearing provided by its huge ears gives it the ability to locate insects perched on leaves in total darkness. It does this partly by echolocation – analysing the echoes of its soft clicking calls to picture its surroundings – but it may also be able to hear the faint sounds made by its prey. Its broad, rounded wings enable it to hover in mid-air as it pinpoints and then seizes an insect.

Bank vole

Although the bank vole is common in Britain, the stumpy, short-tailed mammal is an elusive creature that prefers to stay hidden within the cover of long grass. As the main prey of virtually every native predator, from weasels and foxes to kestrels and owls, it needs to be cautious. Blackberries and other fruits tempt it into bramble thickets and hedges, where it climbs about among the stems, nibbling at the juicy food.

▶ A foraging bank vole may emerge into the open, but by daylight it usually stays in the shade, where it is safer.

Fallow deer

The parks surrounding many ancestral houses often support herds of fallow deer. Although usually shy creatures, in the autumn mating season – known as the rut – the bucks (males) make their presence evident by noisily competing for control of does (females) in breeding condition. Snorting and strutting, they show off their magnificent broad-bladed antlers and thrash them against trees to display their virility. Rivals often fight, charging each other and locking antlers in furious trials of strength. Eventually, one retires defeated and the victor mates with all the does in the harem.

▶ Distracted by an intruder, two fallow bucks take a break from a stand-off that may end in a clash of antlers.

Slow-worm

The slow-worms that live in many parks feed intensively in autumn, to build up their energy reserves. Adult females bear their young in late summer, and slip into hibernation just a few weeks later, in October, so they do not have long to regain peak condition. They hunt insects, spiders, worms and especially small slugs, which they find in the grass or the soil under logs and stones. Meanwhile, the new-born baby slow-worms must also feed well if they are to gain enough weight to survive the long, cold winter.

▲ Its dark stripes show that this slow-worm is a female, searching through the grass for prey in early autumn.

◄ Adult dragonflies, such as this southern hawker, cannot survive the winter, but they keep hunting for as long as possible in autumn.

► Hovering on whirring wings like a hummingbird, a convolvulus hawk-moth sips nectar from a flower at twilight.

Southern hawker

Many dragonflies disappear by late summer, but a few species stay on the wing well into autumn. They include the powerful southern hawker, one of the species most commonly found in parks and gardens in England and Wales. Southern hawkers patrol ponds and woodland glades, flying back and forth at roughly waist height on regular beats, and seizing any small airborne insects they can find. The males in particular are very inquisitive, and anyone walking through their territory is likely to be treated to a close inspection.

Convolvulus hawk-moth

At dusk, a stealthy visitor may be attracted to the park – the convolvulus hawk-moth. This magnificent creature has one of the largest wingspans of any British moth – up to 125mm (5in) – and a powerful flight to match, migrating all the way from southern Europe each year. Its tongue, or proboscis, is twice the length of its body and it uses this to probe long-tubed flowers, and sip nectar that other insects cannot reach. Since it targets these flowers, it carries pollen directly from one long-tubed bloom to the next, ensuring efficient pollination.

Speckled bush cricket

Most bush crickets are out and about in October and even November. They include the oak bush cricket, which has wings, and the sturdier but effectively wingless speckled bush cricket. Both are quite small, mainly green insects with long hind legs and the extremely long, slender antennae that distinguish bush crickets from grasshoppers. Mature females have blade-like appendages, called ovipositors, through which they lay their eggs. The females slip the eggs into bark crevices where they remain until they hatch the following spring.

◄ This female speckled bush cricket may be looking for a site to lay her eggs, using her curved, blade-like ovipositor.

WILDLIFE WATCH

How can I see parkland animals in autumn?

● Try to arrive as early as possible on unfenced common or parkland, or as soon as a park opens, before too many people are about. Animals such as deer tend to be most active around dawn, and the autumn mists and early frosts can make a sighting especially memorable.

● Sometimes in early autumn, parks are open after sunset for special events, such as concerts, and it is possible to watch for owls, hunting bats or foraging moths.

● Investigate the remoter corners of the park, away from the flower beds and play areas. The more neglected areas usually have the richest wildlife.

Black-headed gull

Big open spaces, such as playing fields, are often adopted by large flocks of gulls that move inland to feed in autumn. The most numerous are the small black-headed gulls – although by October most will have lost their dark head plumage. They are slender, graceful birds, but so common that most people barely spare them a glance. They owe their success to their adaptability, since they eat a wide range of foods and have learned to exploit urban landscapes, moving farther inland every year. They spend each night on coasts and lake shores, flying back to their roosts in the early evening in loose, lazy 'V' formations.

▲ A boat on a park lake makes a perfect roosting site for a group of black-headed gulls. In autumn they moult their dark chocolate-brown hoods, leaving just a dark spot behind each eye.

Westonbirt Arboretum – spectacular colours

Famous for its internationally important collection of exotic maples, Westonbirt presents a green landscape of giant trees and delicate foliage, which is transformed by October into a blaze of bronze and red.

An autumn visit to Westonbirt is a memorable experience. It starts with the chill of an overnight frost, which is still lying in the blue shadows as the morning sun burns off the mist in the valley below Silk Wood. The frost gives a snap to the air that mingles with an altogether more earthy scent – a compound

Magnificent mature trees frame the glowing autumn foliage of the maples in Acer Glade, part of the original arboretum at Westonbirt.

of soil, fungi, damp vegetation and fallen leaves. This is the smell of autumn, to be savoured in any deciduous woodland as the days shorten and the leaves change colour and fall.

At Westonbirt the aroma has a peculiar significance, for the fallen leaves are not the usual mixture of russets, browns and yellows. They lie in dazzling drifts of fiery orange, deep crimson, peach, gold and copper. Illuminated by the low autumn sun, those that remain hanging from the branches of oriental plane,

Persian ironwood, hickory and, above all, maple, are simply breathtaking.

The word arboretum means a collection of trees but Westonbirt is much more than that. Originally conceived as a pleasure garden on a grand scale rather than a scientific enterprise, the trees were planted with an eye to how they would look, and not how they were classified by botanists. Many are rare – some were probably the only specimens in Britain when the earliest of them were planted in the 1830s – yet

rarity and novelty were never allowed to override aesthetic considerations as the arboretum was laid out by its original owners, the Holford family. The result is a wooded landscape, where delicacy and majesty complement each other in a symphony of colour and form that reaches its dramatic climax in autumn.

Maple glades

Like most temperate broad-leaved trees, maples react to the onset of winter by cutting off the nutrient supply to their leaves, prior to losing them

HISTORY OF THE ARBORETUM

During the 19th century, professional plant hunters were introducing many new tree species to Britain. On the Westonbirt estate, alkaline soil overlying Jurassic limestone was punctuated by outcrops of acid sand, especially in the area now known as Savill Glade, and this combination was ideal for a huge range of species. The first imported trees were planted in 1829 at the instigation of Robert Holford, the landowner's son, and by 1855 much of the Old Arboretum had been laid out according to the 'picturesque' principles that were fashionable at the time.

Robert's son George is credited with the introduction of the Japanese maples in 1875. He also promoted expansion of the arboretum across the valley into Silk Wood in the 1870s, clearing some of the original woodland

to create several broad rides lined with ornamental trees. After his death in 1926 the estate was split up, and the arboretum suffered 30 years of neglect before being handed over to the Forestry Commission in 1956.

After five years of restoration work, the 240-hectare (600-acre) site was opened to the public as one of two National Arboreta (the other is Bedgebury Pinetum in Kent). Today Westonbirt has one of the world's most important collections of trees and shrubs, with more than 18,500 specimens of almost 3700 different species, varieties and cultivars from all over the world.

► Carefully aligned to provide a superb view from Westonbirt House, Holford Ride passes right through the heart of the Old Arboretum.

altogether. This prevents the formation of chlorophyll, the green pigment that enables leaves to capture the sun's energy and use it to make a form of sugar that the tree uses as food. As the green chlorophyll fades, it reveals yellow, orange and gold pigments called carotenoids that were present throughout the summer.

This happens with all temperate deciduous trees, creating the autumn russets of native oak and beech woods. In maples another process comes into play. Sugars trapped in the cells may stimulate the production of pigments called anthocyanins, which turn the leaves red, scarlet or purple. This creates the dazzling autumn colour seen in Japan and New England, where maples are native trees.

At Westonbirt, one of the first maples to show this effect is the Japanese full-moon maple *Acer japonicum* 'Vitifolium'. In a good year a single tree displays every shade of autumn colour, from green through clear yellow to gold, scarlet and deep wine-red. It is a stunning sight, and an indicator of the show to come, for if the colours are particularly vivid the other maples are sure to follow suit as the season advances. Most of these are cultivars of another Japanese maple, *Acer palmatum*, which has more delicately shaped leaves with fewer lobes. Their variety of leaf form and colour is displayed to full advantage in the original Acer Glade of the Old Arboretum.

Some of these mature trees still survive, supplemented by later plantings both in the original glade and in a more recent Acer Glade, created by the Forestry Commission. Extending for more than 200m (650ft), the new Acer Glade consists of maples propagated from the original trees. They are planted among larch and pine trees to provide the dappled shade and shelter that they would enjoy in Japan, and to accentuate the delicacy of their foliage.

Over in Silk Wood – the larger, wilder tract of woodland that forms the

western part of the site – two more areas have been planted with Japanese maple. One of them, the Link, which dates from the late 1970s, has already developed an informal beauty of its own, while the official National Collection of Japanese maple cultivars has more than 180 different varieties, showcasing the astonishing diversity of this exquisite species.

Specimen trees

Maples are not the only trees that grow at Westonbirt, however. Several of the most spectacular autumn highlights

◄ The delicate, richly coloured foliage of the Japanese maple *Acer palmatum* is a recurring theme at Westonbirt.

▲ Full-moon maple is a variety of *Acer japonicum*, with less finely cut foliage, but equally dazzling autumn colour.

BIRDS AT WESTONBIRT

The greatest variety of bird species occurs in the wilder, less disturbed areas of oak and coppiced hazel in Silk Wood, where the native flora encourages a flourishing insect population. Insects are vital for the young of most woodland birds – even those that are seed-eaters when adult – and the carefully conserved native woodlands at Westonbirt act as a perfect breeding reserve.

In spring and summer they ring with the songs of resident species such as blackbirds, song thrushes, wrens, great tits, marsh tits, chaffinches and greenfinches. These birds are joined by summer visitors such as blackcaps, garden warblers, willow warblers, chiffchaffs, turtle doves, spotted flycatchers, cuckoos, and the occasional tree pipit and pied flycatcher. Some fall prey to

the high-speed aerial attacks of sparrowhawks and, at night, hunting tawny owls.

In autumn and winter both the native and exotic trees provide food for a wide range of forest specialists, including nuthatches, treecreepers, great spotted woodpeckers and the elusive, sparrow-sized lesser spotted woodpecker. Tiny goldcrests and coal tits forage among the conifers, and

gangs of long-tailed tits flit from tree to tree in search of insect eggs and tiny spiders. Crossbills and siskins are sometimes to be seen feeding in the tops of the conifers.

Fruiting shrubs and trees provide food for bullfinches and winter-visiting redwings and fieldfares, and occasionally a crop of berries will attract a nomadic flock of waxwings.

▲ A sporadic visitor from Scandinavia, the waxwing is attracted to autumn berries.

► Goldcrests feed up in the conifers, and draw attention with their shrill calls.

are contributed by quite different trees, such as the sweet gum or liquidamber, the Persian ironwood and the Japanese katsura. Fine examples of all three grow in the Colour Circle near the Acer Glades – an area planted for autumn colour by the original owners, who would invite their friends to 'Colour Circle parties' to appreciate its beauty. The katsura is also notable for its scent, reminiscent of caramel.

Other autumn glories include the multi-hued witch hazels, the rich yellow foliage of big-bud hickory, and the spindle trees with their crimson leaves and bright pink seed capsules. The witch hazels are also wonderful in winter, when

they somewhat perversely burst into bloom with fragrant yellow flowers that last from December to March.

Huge trees are another feature of Westonbirt, including a stupendous Indian cedar and a magnificent Douglas fir. The latter was brought to Britain by the great

◄ Some of the giant redwoods that now rise high above Westonbirt were grown from the first seeds brought to England in 1853.

► In early summer the Chinese pocket-handkerchief tree is festooned with the papery white bracts that surround its small flowers.

◄ Azaleas and camellias flourish on the acid soils of Savill Glade, where the first trees of the arboretum were planted in 1829.

▼ The small-leaved lime is one of the ancient native trees of Britain. The bushy shape shows this one has been coppiced to form a multi-stemmed shrub.

professional plant collector, explorer and botanist David Douglas, who introduced many plants from North America in the early 19th century and may have inspired the creation of the arboretum. The superb Monterey pine at the junction of Circular and Main Drives was grown from one of the original seeds brought back by Douglas from California. The biggest tree of all is a giant redwood, soaring 45m (150ft) high.

Westonbirt has some 130 trees that are 'champions' of their kind – either the tallest or broadest examples of a species in Britain. Ernest Wilson, another famous plant hunter, introduced more than 1000 species from China between 1899 and 1905, including the spectacular pocket-handkerchief tree. The tallest one in Britain can be seen on Main Drive. It is at its best in early summer, when it unfolds the brilliant white bracts for which it is famed.

As the pocket-handkerchief tree fades, attention shifts to two equally exotic introductions from North America, the catalpa with its showy blooms and big leaves, and the tulip tree with its curious four-lobed leaves and solitary, cupped flowers. Another summer-flowering beauty is the Indian horse chestnut, with its almost orchid-like inflorescences surrounded by dark olive-green leaves. Earlier in the year the arboretum is illuminated by the massed blooms of camellias, azaleas and rhododendrons growing on the acid sands of Savill Glade, north of the visitor centre, and Sand Earth in the south-east corner of Silk Wood.

Ancient oaks and limes

Although the arboretum is primarily a collection of exotic trees, it is also notable for its native trees and herbaceous plants, and the wildlife they support. Silk Wood in particular has been a woodland for at least 600 years, and although some parts of it have been replanted with exotics, many areas remain semi-natural woodland, dominated by tall oaks with an understorey of coppiced hazel. These are among the largest areas of such woodland left at Westonbirt, and the acreage is being increased by restoring several areas that were cleared of trees some 60 years ago.

The oldest tree at Westonbirt is not an oak, however, but a small-leaved lime, a species that dominated the wildwood of prehistoric England. A patch of lime coppice in Silk Wood forming a ring of about 80 separate trunks is now known to have developed from a single ancient tree, estimated to be 2000 years old. Coppicing, or the repeated cutting of trees to make them sprout new growth, has the effect of

► A superb Indian cedar soars over the Old Arboretum. Like all cedars, this Himalayan species has fragrant timber.

▲ Tier upon tier of glorious red, orange and yellow autumn foliage make a breathtaking sight during October and early November.

AUTUMN FUNGI

The mild, damp days of autumn are high season for fungi, which burst up from the ground almost overnight to spread their spores. Nearly 1000 species have been recorded at Westonbirt – a total that reflects both the variety of habitats and the wide range of plant species found there. Most fungi live in association with particular green plants, including trees, so more types of plants means more opportunities for fungi.

Among them are several scarce species, such as the vividly coloured devil's bolete, *Boletus satanas*. This is a poisonous relative of the penny bun bolete, or cep, a highly prized edible fungus, which also grows at Westonbirt. Another rarity is *Russula borealis*, one of 57 *Russula* species recorded there. The most threatened species is *Sparassis laminosa*, a cabbage-like fungus that grows on oak. It is listed as endangered, and is a rare find.

▶ A magnificent growth of *Sparassis laminosa* sprouts from the base of an old oak tree at Westonbirt.

▼ A clump of parasol mushrooms spread their broad, scaly caps beneath the trees in a quiet woodland glade.

increasing their potential lifespan – apparently indefinitely in this case. The importance of such trees has been recognised at Westonbirt by the creation of a Native Tree Time Trail in Silk Wood. Along the trail, information panels, audio information and sculptures draw attention to native trees that have been planted chronologically, according to when they are thought to have arrived in Britain in the wake of the last Ice Age.

Grassland orchids

The wilder parts of the arboretum have a rich ground flora, including many wild herbaceous plants that have become scarce elsewhere. These include orchids such as the green-winged orchid, bird's-nest orchid, bee orchid, greater butterfly orchid and violet helleborine. Several of these grow on open chalky grassland between the Old Arboretum and Silk Wood, which has not been ploughed or fertilised for at least 200 years and retains native plants typical of ancient pasture. In shadier woodlands, wild lilies include Solomon's seal and lily-of-the-valley. Wild daffodil and herb-paris thrive.

▲ Orange-tip butterflies lay their eggs on cuckooflower. The eggs hatch into tiny caterpillars that grow rapidly as they eat.

Many areas are awash with bluebells and wood anemones in spring, before the spreading tree canopy shades the woodland floor.

Native plants are vital for insects, especially butterflies. The horseshoe vetch and bird's-foot trefoil that grow on the unspoilt grassland are essential food plants for downland butterflies such as the common blue. Patches of cuckooflower growing in damp corners are sought by orange-tips. Dead wood left standing or lying on the ground in Silk Wood provides food for moth caterpillars, beetles and sawfly grubs. The flourishing insect life attracts insectivorous birds, such as woodpeckers, treecreepers

▶ In autumn, the fragrant white flowers of lily-of-the-valley give way to small berries that glow red among the fallen leaves on the woodland floor.

and flycatchers, and flocks of seed-eating finches and fruit-feeding thrushes roam the woodlands in winter.

The original creators of Westonbirt Arboretum were planning for the future, and since their time it has grown into a world-class collection of magnificent mature trees that draws more than 350,000 visitors a year. For many of these people, the experience is hugely enhanced by the many wild plants, insects and birds that flourish among the trees and on the grassland. They ensure that a trip to Westonbirt offers not just a chance to admire some beautiful trees, but an insight into the complexity of the natural world.

Places to visit at Westonbirt

Glorious autumn colour makes a visit to Westonbirt especially rewarding at this time of year, but its magnificent collection of flowering trees and shrubs also put on a wonderful show throughout the spring and summer. In winter the majesty of the specimen trees and the vivid colours of young dogwood and willow provide a dramatic spectacle, especially when the form of every branch is delineated by a crisp icing of snow.

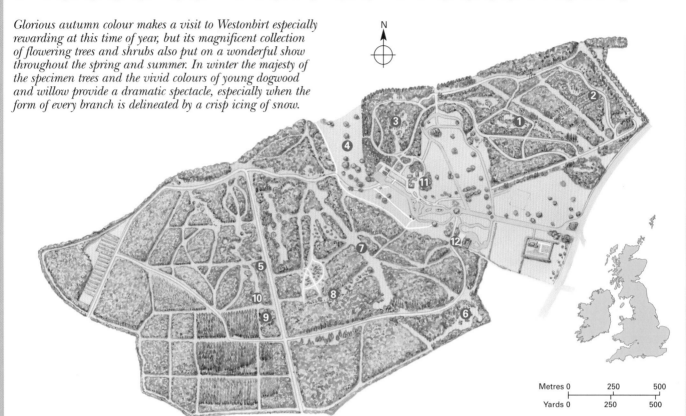

Metres 0 | 250 | 500
Yards 0 | 250 | 500

1 Acer Glades and Colour Circle
The most famous maples in Britain can be seen in all their autumn glory here in the Old Arboretum, as well as many other trees with magnificent autumn colour such as Persian ironwood, witch hazel and katsura.

2 Lime Avenue
In this formal planting of hybrid limes, the flowering trees fill the air with fragrance in summer, and are alive with bees and other insects gathering nectar.

3 Savill Glade and Circular Drive
This is the original 19th-century arboretum. Today many of the trees planted then still tower overhead, while camellias, azaleas and rhododendrons bloom in profusion in spring.

4 The Downs
This tract of open chalky grassland has probably never been treated with herbicides or fertilisers, and is bright with wild flowers and butterflies in spring and summer.

5 Silk Wood
Encompassing the whole of the western part of the site, Silk Wood is where the biggest trees at the arboretum may be seen. It also has the Native Tree Time Trail.

6 Sand Earth
This part of Silk Wood derives its name from its deep sandy soils and is a treasury of acid-loving plants, such as spring-flowering rhododendrons and majestic conifers.

7 Palmer Ride
The long open ride through Silk Wood retains much of the natural character of ancient oak and hazel woodland. It glows with glades of bluebells and primroses in spring.

8 The Link
Planted with maples in the 1970s, the Link is glorious in both spring and autumn, and a good place to enjoy the beauty of the trees in relative peace and quiet.

9 National Japanese Maple Collection
Visit this collection of recently planted maples to marvel at their variety of form and colour.

10 2000-year-old lime
This coppice ring of small-leaved lime in the heart of Silk Wood has developed from an ancient tree that was standing here when the Romans invaded Britain.

11 Visitor centre
Lying between the Old Arboretum and Silk Wood, the visitor centre provides all the usual amenities plus a shop, a café and restaurant overlooking the valley.

12 Plant centre
Many rare and unusual trees are offered for sale, including a selection of Japanese maple cultivars. From spring 2006 these will include two new ones, *Acer palmatum* 'Westonbirt Red' and 'Westonbirt Orange', bred to mark the 50th anniversary of the arboretum coming under the auspices of the Forestry Commission.

How to get there
Westonbirt lies on the A433, roughly 5km (3 miles) south-east of Tetbury. It is 16km (10 miles) north-east of Junction 18 on the M4, and 29km (18 miles) south-east of Junction 13 on the M5. The 620 bus service from Bath to Tetbury stops at the arboretum; it operates from Monday to Saturday, but not Sundays or bank holidays. There is a regular train service to Bath from London and Bristol. For more information, telephone 01666 880220 or visit www.forestry.gov.uk/westonbirt

Opening times
The arboretum is open from 10am to dusk or 8pm, whichever is the earlier, every day of the year. The shop, plant centre and Maples restaurant close at 5pm (closed Christmas Day, Boxing Day and New Year's Day). The Courtyard Café is open from Easter until Christmas. Note that dogs are not permitted in the Old Arboretum, but are permitted in Silk Wood.

Entry fees
The charge for entry is highest in autumn, reflecting the arboretum's popularity at this time, and lowest in winter. Entry is free during the period just before Christmas, after the autumn colour has faded. There are reduced rates for children, senior citizens, students and the disabled. Family tickets are available, and there are concessionary rates for groups of more than 16. For more information, telephone 01666 880220 or visit www.forestry.gov.uk/westonbirt

WILDLIFE WATCH

Where can I see wildlife at Westonbirt?

● Arrive early and head for Silk Wood rather than the prime visitor attractions in the Old Arboretum. Silk Wood is a much more natural habitat that suits birds and other wildlife, and attracts fewer visitors, especially early in the day.

● In autumn and winter, use binoculars to look for canopy-feeding birds such as crossbills and siskins in the tall conifers.

● In spring and summer, explore the grassland of the Downs between the Old Arboretum and Silk Wood. The area has many wild flowers and insects, and attracts birds such as the green woodpecker.

Animals and plants in focus

Garden watch
- The edible dormouse
- Squirrels in the garden
- Swallows and house martins
- The starling
- The chaffinch
- Hoverflies
- Recognising garden spiders
- Garden fungi
- Ragworts and groundsels
- Native trees in the garden

The edible dormouse

Foraging by night in urban gardens and among woodland tree tops, the edible dormouse eats heartily when berries are plentiful. It may even venture into lofts or outbuildings in search of a cosy place to sleep.

With its agile climbing skills, the edible dormouse's small size allows it to venture on to the narrowest branches.

So-named because the Romans kept them in captivity as a good source of fresh meat in winter, edible dormice put on weight in autumn to prepare for hibernation. The Romans fattened up these rodents deliberately, storing them in special earthenware pots that were kept in walled gardens.

A small number of edible dormice, no more than 15, were introduced to Britain from the Continent in 1902 by Walter (later Lord) Rothschild and released in Tring Park, Hertfordshire. They formed a wild breeding population, although a survey conducted in 1995 showed that they had not spread much beyond a 35km (22 mile) radius. The Chilterns are their stronghold in Britain. Edible dormice still thrive in many places on the Continent, from northern Spain and France to east of the Black Sea and north almost as far as the Baltic.

Different dormice

Britain also has a native dormouse, the hazel, or common, dormouse, which is golden yellow and weighs only 10–30g (¼–1oz). By contrast, the edible dormouse is the size of a small squirrel, weighing 200–250g (7–8½oz), and is grey and brown with a white belly and a dark brown tail. While the hazel dormouse inhabits hedges and shrubs in the woodland understorey, the edible dormouse lives mainly in plantations and mature forests, especially beech.

PROTECTED!

Edible dormice are protected under the Berne Convention. The Wildlife and Countryside Act 1981 also forbids trapping edible dormice or releasing them into the wild. Until recently, if the animals were damaging crops, a licence to capture them had to be obtained from the Ministry of Agriculture, but if they were a nuisance in buildings this licence came from the Department of the Environment. English Nature was also to be informed. From 2001, however, the Department for Environment, Food and Rural Affairs (DEFRA) became solely responsible for this licence. Releasing edible dormice into the wild remains illegal.

EDIBLE DORMOUSE FACT FILE

In common with all rodents, the edible dormouse has incisor teeth that grow continually so that frequent gnawing is necessary to keep them in check. Tree bark serves the purpose, as do floorboards and any other wood it may find inside houses.

● **NAMES**
Common names: edible dormouse, fat dormouse, Spanish rat, sleeper, glis
Scientific name: *Glis glis*

● **HABITAT**
Woodland, particularly beech; also orchards and gardens

● **DISTRIBUTION**
Mainly an area within 35km (22 mile) radius of Tring in the Chilterns, but expanding

● **STATUS**
Probably more than 10,000

● **SIZE**
Head and body length 15–17.5cm (6–6½in); tail length 12–15cm (4¾–6in); weight 130–150g (4½–5½oz) rising to 200–250g (7–8¾oz) before hibernation

● **KEY FEATURES**
Grey and brown fur on back, with patches of white especially on belly; long, bushy tail; large black eyes, often with black fur around them; prominent ears; short legs; long, mobile toes; sharp claws

● **HABITS**
Nocturnal, gregarious; family groups begin to break up after about six weeks, but may hibernate together

● **VOICE**
High-pitched squeaks, grunts and churring and wheezing sounds. Calls more likely to be for general communication rather than territorial

● **FOOD**
In summer, flowers and insects, also quite often birds' eggs or nestlings; in autumn, nuts, seeds and fruits

● **BREEDING**
Early August, earlier if breeding in houses or other buildings; litters of up to 11 but usually 2–8; may not breed until third year

● **NEST**
In tree hollows, old squirrel dens, lofts, outbuildings, nesting boxes

● **YOUNG**
Born blind and naked; fur grows within 2 weeks, eyes open by about 3 weeks; leave nest at about a month old; look similar to adults and probably stay close to mother for some time after being weaned

● **SIGNS**
In woods and gardens, crossways stripping of bark from trees; in homes, gnawed woodwork and raided food stores

An edible dormouse spends much of its life asleep, usually below ground where the temperature is low but stable.

Distribution map key

Present all year round

Not present

Sensory organs suited to a nocturnal lifestyle include large ears and eyes, a sensitive nose and long whiskers.

Fur tends to be darkest along the back and around the eyes.

Long, strong toes have needle-sharp claws, allowing a grip on smooth surfaces.

SEASONAL DIET

The edible dormouse's diet varies according to what food is available at the time of year. In spring, as it awakens from hibernation, there are flower buds with nutritious pollen. In summer and autumn, a plentiful supply of flowers gives way to fruit, nuts, fungi and tree bark – especially the juicy layer that lies beneath the dry, flaky outer layers. This essentially vegetarian diet is supplemented with insects, carrion, birds' eggs and even nestlings if the dormouse happens upon them.

A varied diet means that the edible dormouse can take advantage of less natural surroundings, and can do well scavenging in and around houses and gardens where it gnaws rafters and lead pipes, and feasts on berries from fruiting shrubs and trees. Reports of edible dormice living in houses have become increasingly common.

▲ Once a tree has been 'ringed' by the nibbling teeth of the edible dormouse, its crown will soon die. The tops of such trees break off easily in high winds.

Tree-top foraging

In late summer the edible dormouse searches avidly for food, climbing nimbly in the treetops. It needs to eat heartily to prepare for its winter hibernation and may nearly double its summer weight by autumn.

The edible dormouse whisks its large, bushy tail to and fro as it climbs along branches. It uses its tail to balance its body weight, allowing it to use both of its front feet to grab at insects, such as a resting moth.

Tree damage

Living mainly in the high branches of trees, the edible dormouse can cause much damage, chewing bark, buds and shoots. It is particularly partial to the sweet, juicy sapwood found under the bark of fruit and timber trees. For foresters in the Chilterns, the edible dormouse can be a 'pest', although it has never been labelled formally as such.

To the untrained eye, edible dormouse activity in a forest can be easily mistaken for that of a squirrel. Both strip bark but whereas squirrels tear pieces from the tree lengthways, edible dormice rip off the bark sideways, often removing a ring from around the tree. This is damaging because the fine tubes – called xylem and phloem – that transport water and nutrients up and down the tree are just under the bark. If the tubes are torn, the top of the tree is cut off from its water supply, and the base is starved of the carbohydrates made in the leaves. An apparently small amount of damage can prove fatal for a tree.

Moving population

In the past, residents in the Chilterns used humane traps to capture edible dormice, releasing them as far away as possible, in order to prevent them invading their houses and gardens. The problem with that short-term solution was that more dormice moved in to fill the space. Now edible dormice are protected, so trapping and releasing them without a licence is illegal.

Moving these tree-dwelling dormice has allowed them to cross natural barriers created by areas of open land, such as the Vale of Aylesbury. While it is difficult to trace where they have been liberated, there is evidence of at least one release 100km (62 miles) from Tring. At present, there are at least 10,000 edible dormice in Britain and probably many more. In 1991, a study of the Chiltern population, using their distinctive calls, estimated that edible dormice live, on average, one or two per hectare (2½acres).

Dormice need a plentiful supply of food each autumn to help them build up the reserves to survive a six or seven-month hibernation. Sugar-rich fruits and fatty nuts are ideal for putting on extra weight.

Nocturnal activity

Edible dormice, like hazel dormice, are active at night. Both males and females have a range of calls, varying from high-pitched squeaks to grunts and loud churring and wheezing sounds. These calls are most likely to be used for general communication rather than for defending territories. The dormice continue to make them well after the breeding season has finished. Humans may be alerted to the presence of edible dormice by the noise the animals make as they call to one another in the tree tops. Another occasion when humans may be made aware of their presence is if the rodents get into the house and scurry about overhead in the loft, preparing to hibernate.

Edible dormice spend most of their waking hours foraging in tree tops. In common with the hazel dormouse, they rely on food that varies with the seasons, and particular types of woodland provide them with an abundant food supply. Areas where there are plenty of beech trees, especially where beech and spruce trees grow together, are the edible dormouse's most successful breeding grounds. This is because such a combination provides a rich source of flowers, cones and nuts, as well as a large number of aphids and other insects. Beech trees, mixed with plantations of spruce and larch, are prevalent in the Chilterns, perhaps explaining why the edible dormouse thrives in this area but breeds less successfully in others.

Returning to favoured feeding sites each night until the available food has been eaten up, edible dormice then move on. They are adept climbers, having fingers and toes that grip so well that they can climb and make spectacular leaps in near-total darkness.

Long hibernation

By late autumn, food in the tree tops is scarce and edible dormice spend more time foraging on the ground, where they will also usually search for holes in which to hibernate. The last few weeks of the summer season are a race to put on enough weight to survive the winter hibernation. This is especially challenging for the young of late litters. Those that survive tend to develop comparatively slowly and do not breed until their third summer.

The edible dormouse settles down to sleep in its nest when the first frost chills the air. To save energy, its body

▲ Individual fur colour varies considerably, but true albinos, such as this one, are rare. Not only is the fur white, but the eyes lack the black pigment that usually masks the blood-red tissues beneath.

'DORMICE ATE MY HOUSE'

When this headline appeared in a local Hertfordshire newspaper, it came as no surprise to the inhabitants of Tring and the surrounding area. Edible dormice are often reported in houses, where they can create disturbance and cause considerable damage. The presence of edible dormice in the loft is said to produce a level of noise akin to having a football team overhead at night when humans are attempting to sleep!

When Hertfordshire residents were questioned, a variety of edible dormouse tales were forthcoming.

A total of 65 edible dormice were removed from one house by pest control officers. Another resident told of edible dormice feeding on elderberries from the garden before spending the night in the airing cupboard and producing a mess of purple droppings.

In Aston Clinton, edible dormice gnawed through an organ pipe at the parish church. They were also blamed for gnawing the wires in a Rolls-Royce. A factory owner reported edible dormice running around at night and regularly setting off the burglar alarms.

Edible dormice can adapt to living anywhere that provides them with enough food – in particular, fruit – and are often found in orchards and gardens. Hazel dormice prefer a thick tangle of woodland scrub.

NESTBOXES

In the Chilterns more than a hundred nestboxes have been put up in woodland so that new information can be gathered on edible dormice, in particular their breeding habits. The animals have customised their boxes by gnawing the entrance holes to size.

Litter sizes vary but are usually between two and eight. Naked at first, the young are soon covered in fur, grey on the back with a white underside.

Animals found in nestboxes are categorised into three distinct groups according to their weight. Those weighing less than 50g (1½oz) are nestlings. Well-grown juveniles (young of the previous year) usually weigh 70–130g (2½–4⅝oz) while active adults weigh 130–150g (4⅝–5½oz) rising to 200–250g (7–8¾oz) after building up fat stores in the autumn. Some edible dormice may not breed until after their second birthday, during their third summer.

Nestbox studies have also revealed that two or more edible dormice may choose to share a dry, sheltered nesting site. What appear to be family groups are often found curled up in the nest together.

The young are blind and naked when they are first born, and are totally dependent on their mother. Their fur grows quite quickly, and they will have a full coat by the time they are 16 days old. Their eyes do not open until they are about three weeks old.

temperature goes down and its heart rate and respiratory rate slow. Most edible dormice hibernate for seven months – some a bit less and others more. Remaining torpid for this time gives the edible dormouse its German name, *Siebenschläfer*, meaning 'seven-sleeper'. It lives by using up its fat reserves, losing nearly half its body weight.

Super senses

In its preferred home of deciduous woodland, the edible dormouse uses its highly developed senses of sight, hearing and smell to navigate its way as it forages for food.

Edible dormice often find their way into houses and gardens in search of a dry winter retreat. They may choose to sleep in outbuildings or drainpipes, or under tree roots or floorboards. Temperature is fairly stable underground, which prevents the animals' fat reserves from being used up too rapidly, but if they can't find natural holes, they may

hibernate in groups, perhaps in lofts. More than 50 edible dormice have been discovered occupying a single house.

It is not known for certain if edible dormice ever become torpid in the summer. Hazel dormice sleep to save energy if the weather becomes colder or there is a sudden food shortage. Edible dormice are occasionally found in a cold, lethargic state, so it is possible.

Caring for young

Spending up to seven months or more of each year in hibernation means that the edible dormouse has just five months in which to meet a mate, breed and fatten up young so that they are large enough to survive the winter. Litters born after the end of August are unlikely to survive.

The female produces a single litter in midsummer in a nest in a tree hollow that may be lined with dried leaves and grass, or an old squirrel den or sometimes in corners in lofts. Edible dormice living in trees mostly do not produce young until

Vigilance is essential when leaving the safety of the nest, as a rotund dormouse makes a good meal for an owl as well as predatory stoats and weasels.

WILDLIFE WATCH

Where can I see edible dormice?

● Edible dormice are largely restricted to parts of the Chiltern Hills in Hertfordshire and Buckinghamshire. They are not limited to dense scrub like hazel dormice, nor do they build characteristic nests but have been known to make their homes almost anywhere that has a good food supply.

● As nocturnal animals, edible dormice are more often heard than seen. A walk in the woods after dark in summer may be rewarded with snatches of their churring and wheezing calls. A sighting of one sitting at the entrance to its tree hole or burrow, or scrambling nimbly through the canopy, is then possible.

Tree holes make ideal nesting places but the edible dormouse will nest in almost any secure cavity, including gaps in tree roots, birds' nests, roof spaces and rabbit burrows. They even dig burrows for themselves.

August but those living indoors may produce young earlier. The female feeds her young on milk, and also chews food to a pulp, which she then feeds them direct from her mouth. This encourages them to grow quickly. Weaning occurs at about four weeks, when they leave the nest but usually stay close by. Males probably take no part in rearing young.

In the home

When edible dormice move into homes to live, rather than just hibernate, they gnaw electric wires and woodwork, raid stored food and chew bars of soap. They also establish latrines – in dry, warm places such as lofts and airing cupboards – in which they deposit large quantities of droppings. Edible dormice sometimes drown in lavatory pans and household cisterns, which can result in fur and bones coming out of bathroom taps. Particular houses seem to attract edible dormice, while others nearby are left uninvaded. The reasons for this are unknown.

Getting a grip

When climbing, the edible dormouse spreads its limbs to the side and flattens itself against the trunks of trees, holding on with needle-sharp claws. Hollows in tree trunks provide ideal resting and surveillance places.

The edible dormouse can rotate its hind feet at the ankles to climb downwards like a squirrel.

EDIBLE DORMICE AND SQUIRRELS

Like the squirrel, the edible dormouse is a rodent adapted to life in trees. The great 18th-century Swedish biologist Carl Linnaeus thought that the edible dormouse and the red squirrel were related closely enough to share the scientific name *Sciurus* – the red squirrel is *S. vulgaris* and the edible dormouse was *S. glis*, although this was later changed to *Glis glis*.

Both the squirrel and the edible dormouse have four long mobile toes on each foot, and a vestigial thumb, which gives them an excellent grip. The soles of the edible dormouse's feet have a pattern of pads that provide extra adhesion, allowing it to grip on to surfaces securely. The pads may even have a suction effect by creating a partial vacuum.

Both the squirrel and the edible dormouse use their tails as a counter-balance to stop themselves toppling off precarious perches. As the edible dormouse spends much of its life asleep, curled up in a ball, its furry tail also comes in useful for providing extra warmth, and the animal drapes it over its body.

From a distance, the edible dormouse can be mistaken for a squirrel, although it is smaller and far less likely to descend to the ground.

Squirrels in the garden

Active in daylight, particularly in autumn, the agile grey squirrel searches gardens for nuts and fruit, and often helps itself to food from bird tables and feeders. The red squirrel is a much rarer garden visitor.

A grey squirrel will eat anything it can find on a bird table, from peanuts to apples. Unlike most mammals, squirrels are adept at manipulating food with their front paws.

First introduced to Britain from North America in 1876, the grey squirrel has now far superseded the native red squirrel in nearly all areas of the country. Where food is plentiful, grey squirrels can number more than 16 per hectare (2½ acres). Most red squirrels live in Scotland and Ireland, although some still live in parts of northern England and Wales.

Squirrels frequent urban and country gardens, and gardens close to woodland will almost certainly be visited by them. Performing acrobatics as they search for food, they are assisted by powerful gripping feet with strong claws. Their hind feet can rotate at the ankle, allowing them to climb down trees headfirst and even hang head-down, gripping with their hind claws. Manoeuvrable fingers on their front feet enable squirrels to hold food in their paws, and their sharp teeth open nut shells easily. They use their fingers and tongues to extract the kernels from the sunflower seeds they find in birdfeeders.

Opportunistic eating

Adaptable and resourceful, squirrels are quick to take advantage of birdfeeders. A nut basket intended for birds is a treasure trove for squirrels. They gnaw through the string from which the basket hangs, then devour the nuts spilt as it crashes to the

▼ Its ability to hang upside down allows this grey squirrel to reach a nut basket suspended from a washing line. A strong spine assists the squirrel's agility.

▲ Forward-facing eyes enable the squirrel to judge distances accurately before it takes a leap from a vantage point to attack nut baskets and bird tables.

ground. Using wire instead of string prevents squirrels from using this technique, but they soon learn to leap to the basket from the nearest tree or wall. Then they gnaw away the base of the basket or open its lid. They do, however, have great difficulty climbing around cone-shaped anti-squirrel baffles fitted to bird tables. Red squirrels are less adept than grey ones at breaking into birdfeeders.

Squirrels are inclined to visit gardens in autumn in search of nuts, fruit and seeds, which they may hoard for the winter by burying them. Sometimes they nibble tree bark, but tend to do this only if not enough other food is available to them in winter.

Changes of coat
Squirrels moult their body fur – and in grey squirrels, their tail and ear fur as well – twice each year, in spring and again in

autumn. In the weeks between August and November, the grey squirrel's relatively thin summer coat is replaced by a thicker, more luxuriant winter one. This has a distinctive grizzled, salt–and-pepper appearance. Each hair is banded with grey and yellowish brown, with a white tip. The white tips of the hairs are especially noticeable on the long fur of the bushy tail. In summer the tail looks rather thin and scruffy, but during autumn it becomes neater and bushier in appearance.

The red squirrel's summer coat is bright chestnut, not the khaki-brown seen on parts of the grey squirrel. During autumn, its coat becomes greyer and the red squirrel acquires prominent ear tufts for winter that never occur in grey squirrels.

Nesting in trees
Squirrels may build their nests in garden trees. They usually have two litters each year, produced at any time except for mid-winter. Typically, they have one litter in March or April, and another in June or July. In the warmer south, young may be born as early as January or, in the case of the second litter, as late as September.

▲ As well as foraging in trees, the grey squirrel searches for food on the ground, even on a garden lawn. Feeling less safe here, it sits up to check for danger.

▼ Inquisitive and opportunistic, a squirrel will drink from a bird bath. It pushes itself upwards with its hind legs while its front legs reach over the rim.

The squirrel's long powerful hind legs allow it to make spectacular leaps, while its shorter front legs act as shock absorbers on landing.

WILDLIFE WATCH

How can I attract squirrels to the garden?

● Most nut-producing and fruiting trees entice squirrels into the garden, especially oak, beech, hazel, willow, field maple, hornbeam, ash and sweet chestnut. Pine trees and other conifers attract them as well. Squirrels are most likely to be seen in the garden in autumn when the crops are ripe for eating, or for storing as winter approaches.

● Squirrels may travel more than a kilometre (½ mile) to places where food is provided daily. A food table in winter is especially welcome if the autumn crop of acorns, beech mast and chestnuts has been poor.

Swallows and house martins

Each year swallows and house martins gather on overhead wires before flying off to warmer climes for the winter. They often leave their perches for a short time, circling restlessly and twittering incessantly.

Sometimes seen together hawking for insects over water, swallows and house martins are closely related and resemble each other. Their streamlined silhouettes are similar but the swallow is distinguished by having long tail streamers and more pointed wings than the house martin, which has a distinctive white rump. Both have wings shaped for speed and agility, allowing the birds to catch insects in flight and to complete long journeys south for the winter months.

Gathering in groups

As well as joining swallows on overhead wires, house martins often also gather on south-facing roofs where the tiles soak up heat from the sun, and they use inland cliffs or quarry sides for the same reason. Mostly made up of young birds, these mixed assemblies begin to form in August, although in years when the weather is particularly warm, flocks of house martins may still be seen as late as October.

Roosts and other gatherings offer many advantages to swallows and house martins. Congregations of birds may allow information to spread about the best areas to feed. Hungry new arrivals to the group can perhaps follow the early, better-fed birds as they return to a previously discovered food supply.

Conspicuous gatherings of swallows are sure sign of approaching autumn. They may be noisily obvious one day and gone the next.

NESTS ON CLIFFS

House martins are renowned for plastering their mud nests on to houses, which means that the birds bring up their young in close proximity to humans. While the majority of pairs choose buildings as nest sites, birdwatchers occasionally find numbers of house martins nesting together on cliffs, far away from urban areas. It seems that the sheer faces and overhanging ledges characteristic of cliffs represent the original, natural version of the walls and eaves of buildings usually chosen by the birds.

SWALLOW FACT FILE

A familiar visitor to the rural outskirts of towns and villages, the swallow may be seen in swooping flight, long forked tail much in evidence as it chases its insect prey.

● **NAMES**
Common names: swallow, barn swallow
Scientific name: *Hirundo rustica*

● **HABITAT**
Feeds in open country, especially over lowland mixed farms and waterside pasture; needs buildings for nesting

● **DISTRIBUTION**
Throughout Britain and Ireland but sparse on remote Scottish islands

● **STATUS**
About 570,000 breeding pairs in Britain; up to 250,000 in Ireland; declining

● **SIZE**
Length 17–20cm (6½–8in) including tail streamers, which are 2–7cm (¾–2¾in); weight 16–25g (½–1oz)

● **KEY FEATURES**
Glossy dark blue upperparts with reddish chestnut forehead and throat, dark chest band, whitish to buff underparts and white spots on the underside of tail near where it forks

● **HABITS**
Mostly catches insects in flight, or sometimes picks them off vegetation

● **VOICE**
Male song is sweet twittering warbling mixed with guttural rattling; loud *'tswit tswit'* alarm call

● **FOOD**
Many flies, including hoverflies, also aphids, flying ants, bees, wasps and mayflies

● **BREEDING**
Most arrive in late April–early May, but some earlier in south and later in north; lays eggs from end April; 2, sometimes 3, broods in a season

● **NEST**
Open mud cup, lined with feathers, often attached to rafters or tiny ledges, under a ceiling or roof; several birds may build nests in a single building; often use hides on wetland nature reserves

● **EGGS**
Glossy white with light reddish markings; most clutches 4–6 eggs, 5 most common in first clutch, 4 in second; incubation period about 15 days

● **YOUNG**
Remain in nest for 18–23 days; both parents feed them and continue for about a week after fledging; neighbours may also bring food

In bright sunlight, the head, neck and breast band have a metallic blue sheen.

The back is glossy dark blue.

Although very short legs rule out easy walking on the ground, curved feet provide a good grip on wires and stems.

Deeply forked, the delicate tail streamers are longest in males.

Distribution map key

▨ Present during summer

☐ Not present

HOUSE MARTIN FACT FILE

Well known in most parts of Britain, the house martin is sometimes seen alongside the swallow, although it is more inclined to live in urban areas, where it often builds its nest in house eaves.

● **NAMES**
Common name: house martin
Scientific name: *Delichon urbica*

● **HABITAT**
In and around villages and towns; often feeds over lakes and other fresh water

● **DISTRIBUTION**
Found over most of the country; rare or absent from outermost isles and highest hills

● **STATUS**
Population fluctuates considerably but apparently declining, particularly in south-eastern England; may now be fewer than 200,000

● **SIZE**
Length 12.5–14cm (4¾–5½in); weight 15–20g (½–¾oz)

● **KEY FEATURES**
Smaller and chunkier than the swallow, with similar dark upperparts; white underparts and distinctive white rump; legs feathered

● **HABITS**
Insects caught in flight

● **VOICE**
Song is very quiet and chattering; main call is a hard, scratchy *'prrrit'* or *'prri-tit'*

● **FOOD**
Flying insects, mainly flies and aphids

● **BREEDING**
Nesting starts in May, continuing until last young fledge in October; 2 broods, occasionally 3 in a season

● **NEST**
About the size of a small coconut quarter with a slit entrance; formed from 1000 or more mud pellets, lined with feathers and other material mostly gathered from the air; usually sited under the eaves of buildings, sometimes on cliffs

● **EGGS**
Clutches of 3, 4 or 5 white eggs, usually unmarked; incubated by both parents (more by female); usually hatch after 14–16 days but delayed by bad weather

● **YOUNG**
Remain in the nest for at least 21 days, longer in damp, cool weather; young birds return to nest to rest and roost after fledging; migrant birds may use nests in colonies for roosting

Distribution map key

▨ Present during summer

☐ Not present

In most light conditions and at long range, the head, neck and back appear almost black.

Upperparts have a steely blue sheen.

Although the tail is forked it does not have the long, very narrow streamers of the adult swallow.

The house martin's bill is short and stubby, and the bird uses it as an effective tool for plastering its mud nest on to the outer walls of buildings – a site just under the eaves or on a window frame is favoured.

Birds in a flock are also less likely to become victims of predators. The presence of a hobby or other bird of prey is communicated through special alarm calls and it is confusing for the predator to pick out one bird from the rest while they are in flight. For young birds about to migrate for the first time, gathering together – as well as the journey itself – is a communal activity whereby they learn to live socially, which is important for such gregarious birds.

Flying south

Before cold, wet weather deprives them of their insect prey, swallows and house martins migrate to Africa for the winter. On the way, some house martins may roost overnight in disused nests, but many probably fly around in circles snatching sleep on the wing at high altitudes. They most likely have brief naps as they glide along, perhaps gradually losing height, then wake up and fly higher again. The birds' 'furry feet' – little white feathers cover their legs and toes – ensure heat is retained as they fly in the cold night sky.

Without these feathers, swallows spend the night gathered together in roosts. These are often in reedbeds where the

▶ Parents care for newly hatched swallows for around four weeks. They bring food regularly to the youngsters in the nest for three weeks, and continue to feed them for another week after they have fledged.

▼ A young swallow's plumage is more dowdy than that of adults. The colours are less intense and the tail has much shorter, blunt streamers. A few fluffy, nestling feathers remain.

Demanding food

Young swallows have a large, bright orange gape, which acts as a powerful stimulus for the parents to provide food. The biggest and brightest gapes are the most evident, and parents home in on these conspicuous signals.

Hovering over the young bird as it reaches up to receive a proffered insect, the parent places the food carefully into its offspring's throat.

SWALLOW AND HOUSE MARTIN CALENDAR

NOVEMBER • FEBRUARY

The birds are in their winter quarters – western Africa for house martins and mostly South Africa for swallows. Both species moult during this time and acquire a new, healthy plumage for the return journey to Britain.

MARCH • APRIL

The route includes a hazardous crossing of the Sahara to northern Africa through weather that is often poor. The first birds may appear in Britain from mid-March, but some house martins may not arrive until May or even early June.

MAY

May is a period of diligent nest building, a task that requires an adequate source of wet, sticky mud no more than 200m (650ft) from the nest site. House martins can often be seen gathering in large flocks at good 'mud sites'.

JUNE • JULY

Nestlings call tirelessly for food during daylight hours. When they have fledged, the young birds perch on roofs or similar surfaces that have been warmed by the morning sunlight.

AUGUST

Young house martins start to gather on wires and roofs, from where they explore their local area and prepare to leave. Swallows, too, begin to gather in large flocks.

SEPTEMBER • OCTOBER

Swallows complete the long journey south in a series of short flights between reedbed roosts. House martins take slightly less time by flying continuously, probably sleeping on the wing.

A couple of weeks before migrating, young house martins gather in groups, often in the vicinity of their breeding sites or near water. They spend this time adapting to living independently from their parents.

relative warmth of the water below the birds helps to keep them warm at night, and is a barrier to ground predators. On their journey south, swallows find reedbeds throughout Europe and Africa.

Herald of spring

Swallows and house martins return to Britain from March – the swallow has even become a traditional herald of spring. Farmland where nearby water provides insect prey is favoured by swallows after their tiring journey. The birds tend to feed heartily, exhausting one food supply, and then move on. A river with plenty of mayflies, for example, might be favoured for a time before it is abandoned for a site where other insects have emerged.

House martins are more likely than swallows to live near humans, in and around villages, towns and even big cities such as London. Like swallows, they prey on aerial insects and find good feeding opportunities wherever there is water, including reservoirs, farmland and woodland. As they hawk for insects, swallows and house martins share impressive hunting skills. They are able to execute nimble changes of direction to catch their prey. This concentration on feeding is vital in spring, as the birds rebuild their condition after their journey and before breeding.

Breeding pairs

It was once believed that swallows and house martins formed monogamous pairs to breed, especially when they nest some distance apart. While this is mostly the case, all the chicks in a single brood are not necessarily fathered by the same male. When swallows and house martins nest in colonies, they often mate with additional birds as well as their original partners. For males there is the advantage that any

Swoop and glide

Swallows are superb aerial hunters, specialising in hawking for flying insects. Characteristically, the birds fly very low over fields and water, where they will also drink and bathe on the wing. They may make repeated trips to areas where prey is plentiful, sometimes circling overhead.

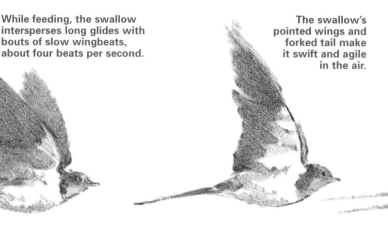

While feeding, the swallow intersperses long glides with bouts of slow wingbeats, about four beats per second.

The swallow's pointed wings and forked tail make it swift and agile in the air.

extra chicks allow even more of their genes to be carried into the next generation. For females, extra matings offer more chance of a healthy chick in case their original choice of mate was poor – for example, an impotent male or one that produces weak offspring.

Females tend to choose males with the longest tail streamers, and these are an eye-catching feature of adult males as they return in spring. Along with a distinctive song, the tail streamers indicate that the first birds back are males. The females return, on average, about a week later. Pairs then spend 10 days to a fortnight building new nests. If a pair have the

good fortune to discover an old nest that is still complete and available, the female may lay eggs before the end of April. However, if the weather is cold and wet, or if the female arrives back in poor condition, the clutch may not be laid until the end of May.

Wet mud

Both swallows and house martins collect glutinous mud with which to build their nests. As they fly back to nest sites, the mud dries out in their beaks, so they collect mud that is wetter than they need. After about 200m (650ft) of flight, even the soggiest mud pellets become too dry.

Any nest site more than this distance from mud is therefore of no use unless there is an old nest or nestbox already in place. In hot weather when puddles dry up, nest building becomes challenging for swallows and house martins. The absence of these birds from some urban areas where most surfaces are covered in tarmac may be partly due to the absence of mud for nests. Providing clay mud by keeping puddles moist, or even creating muddy puddles – in an old washing up bowl or sink in the garden – is a good conservation measure for the birds when they are busy plastering their nests in spring, particularly if the weather

When it comes to feeding time, each chick clamours to be fed first. In this competition between siblings, the strongest chick invariably wins.

DID YOU KNOW?

In winter, the majority of swallows that nest in Britain can be found in South Africa. British house martins also head for sub-Saharan Africa, where they settle over a wide area. It is thought that droughts in their wintering quarters may be at least partly responsible for a decline in both the swallow and house martin populations, since a lack of rain results in fewer insects on which to feed.

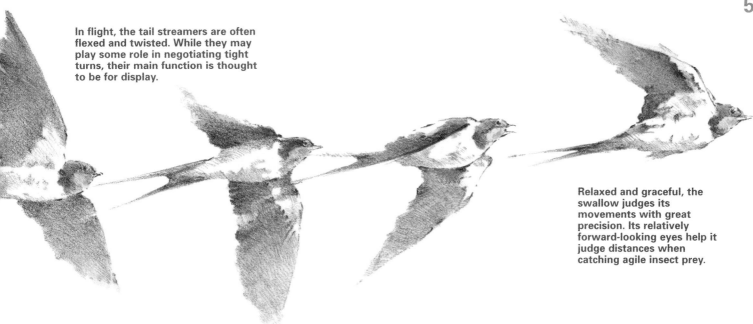

In flight, the tail streamers are often flexed and twisted. While they may play some role in negotiating tight turns, their main function is thought to be for display.

Relaxed and graceful, the swallow judges its movements with great precision. Its relatively forward-looking eyes help it judge distances when catching agile insect prey.

is more than usually dry or there is a drought. It can also be helpful to pour a couple of buckets of water over earth in a suitable place – perhaps on a bare patch of lawn or even outside the garden in a dusty country lane.

There are several records of instances when house martins have tried to build nests using very sandy soil with poor results. The dry soil crumbled away on to the ground beneath the nest site. The best mud tends to be found around field gateways, trampled and churned up by cattle, or to come from muddy puddles, or the edges of ponds and streams rather than undisturbed wet earth.

Fortunately, both swallows and house martins take readily to nestboxes made from clay-like material or sometimes even coconuts and plastic. The presence of artificial nests may also entice other birds to build their own nearby. Further encouragement comes from providing suitable nest materials, such as straw, which will be collected enthusiastically by the birds.

Caring community

House martins may feed the young in adjacent nests if their own are not begging, and sometimes parents of broods that have not yet hatched will bring food to their neighbour's young. Newly hatched birds may get their first feed after just two hours.

Generally, in a colony of a dozen or so nests, the birds are very involved with each other. The most intense activity takes place when the young are about to fledge – parents and neighbours rush about in what appears to be an attempt at enticing the young birds out.

In autumn, a very small number of hybrids between swallows and house martins may appear. If the opportunity arises, it is clear that an over-eager male may mount the wrong female. Just a few

of these young hybrid birds have been recorded in a single autumn in Britain, and sadly, there are no records of any surviving to return in the spring.

Stolen nests

Nests built by swallows and house martins are often used in following years by other birds. Wrens, robins and spotted flycatchers are all known to recycle old swallow's nests. House martin nests are used in winter by roosting blue tits and wrens, sometimes by a dozen or more. The nests are not large enough for other tits to roost in, but the miniature wren sometimes adopts them permanently.

House sparrows also usurp house martin nests in winter. Entrances to the nests are too small for sparrows so they chip away to enlarge them. They may even hijack nests while house martins are building them in spring, timing their take-over before the entrance becomes too narrow.

WILDLIFE WATCH

Where can I see swallows and house martins?

● During autumn swallows and house martins gather on overhead wires, often the same ones each year. These sociable birds are almost all youngsters but some failed breeders also form part of the group.

● To see migrating swallows and house martins, head for eastern and southern coasts. Check the weather forecast for a fine day with a northerly breeze. In these conditions the birds will fly low to avoid the stronger winds at higher altitudes.

● House martin nests can be seen on the outside of buildings under the eaves. The nests consist of an enclosed mud cup positioned on a rafter or ledge, and are often found in groups of three or four, sometimes a few more. Larger house martin colonies of dozens of pairs of birds are now rare.

● Swallows tend to nest inside outbuildings, such as barns and stables – in North America they are known as barn swallows. Garages and porches are also used.

● When the weather is cool or windy, the birds may forage farther away from their nest sites. Dense flocks – including sand martins and unrelated swifts – can form over water. The water retains heat and often many insects hatch from the shallows, providing the birds with food.

● In spring, the first birds to return are likely to be seen on a blustery day at a lake, reservoir or gravel pit, snapping up early insects.

The starling

Pale-spotted, blackish feathers shot with iridescence, a short tail and a jerky walk help make the starling easily recognisable. In autumn, resident birds are joined by millions of visitors from colder parts of eastern Europe.

A sociable bird, the starling is notorious for descending in hordes to demolish bird food and kitchen scraps intended for more timid and delicate garden birds. Its bold nature also allows it to take advantage of food provided by agricultural land. Thousands of starlings may raid corn crops, leaving the corn stripped bare. More beneficially, they eat agricultural pests such as leatherjackets – even searching for insects within the fur of livestock.

Not all the starlings visiting gardens in autumn and winter have spent the year in Britain – many have just completed a lengthy journey. From October to early April, the starlings scavenging in British gardens are as likely to have been born in Poland, Norway, Estonia or Finland as in the next-door shrubbery. The warming influence of the Gulf Stream keeps winter temperatures in Britain higher than those of countries farther to the east. In eastern Europe, the winters are long, frozen and snowbound. In an attempt to avoid the hardships of freezing weather and scarce food, millions of birds fly west or south for the winter months. They join the thousands of starlings that live in Britain all year round.

In the breeding season, starlings are resplendent with glossy plumage and a yellow beak. They frequently nest in the eaves of houses and also use nestboxes.

Bird baths in gardens attract starlings. Like other birds, they need water not only for drinking but for bathing, which is important for keeping their feathers in good condition.

There is no evident difference in appearance between the foreign visitors and resident starlings. However, the song of a particular bird will often betray its origins. Starlings have their own song but are also excellent mimics of other birds. Those that mimic the distinctive calls of the curlew or redshank, for example, have probably been reared in marshlands, uplands or near the coast, while the liquid whistles of the golden oriole may indicate a starling reared on the Continent – the oriole breeds in very small numbers in Britain, almost all in East Anglia.

Winter-visiting starlings return to their homelands for the summer to breed and rear their young. In many European countries, spring starlings are welcomed as heralds of summer, and large numbers of nestboxes are erected for their use. In other areas, they are looked upon as pests, liable to descend in great numbers on cherry orchards as the fruit ripens.

STARLING FACT FILE

A small to medium-sized bird, the starling has glossy dark plumage, studded with pale spots, especially in winter. It is gregarious and, when not breeding, congregates in large numbers to form noisy roosts in urban areas throughout Britain.

● NAMES
Common names: starling, European starling
Scientific name: *Sturnus vulgaris*

● HABITAT
Gardens and farmland

● DISTRIBUTION
Throughout Britain and Ireland except mountains of north-western Scotland; sparse in far western Wales and Cornwall

● STATUS
Common, but probably fewer than 700,000 breeding pairs in Britain and 250,000–500,000 in Ireland; major decline in the past 30 years or so

● SIZE
Length 21.5cm (8½in); weight 75–90g (2¾–3¼oz)

● KEY FEATURES
Adults black with glossy purple and green feathers – most obvious on head and breast in adult males; beak sharp and slightly curved, yellow in breeding season, dark brownish in winter

● HABITS
Flocks in large numbers to feeding sites, including rubbish tips, fast-food outlets, cattle feeders, orchards and garden feeders; often digs in grass for invertebrates

● VOICE
Very vocal at all times of year, except males during late summer moult; fluting whistles, clicks, gurgles and competent mimicry of other sounds, including other bird calls, telephones, door chimes and car alarms; most common call is a loud, grating *'tcheerr'* often used as an alarm call

● FOOD
Omnivorous; natural foods include apples, cherries, caterpillars, leatherjackets and flying ants

● BREEDING
First eggs typically laid early April, last young fledge in late July; some have 2 broods

● NEST
Usually in a tree hole sited up to 15m (50ft) from ground; also in cavities on houses and in cliffs; occasionally on ground; huge quantities of nest material gathered for large holes; largest nests may be as much as 1m (3ft) across

● EGGS
Pale unmarked blue, glossy; average clutch usually 4–6 eggs; first clutches bigger than replacements or second attempts; both adults incubate but female takes the greater share; incubation lasts about 12 days

● YOUNG
Mousy grey-brown feathering and dark beak; fledge in about 21 days; gradually moult to adult plumage in late summer and autumn; have jerky gait

Dark during the winter months, the beak becomes lemon yellow in the breeding season.

Buffish brown spots usually mark the crown and upperparts.

In winter the glossy breast is marked with pale spots on the tips of the feathers.

The tail is short compared with that of the blackbird and other thrushes, and the wing and tail feathers are dark with pale margins.

Distribution map key

Present all year round

Not present

STARLING CALENDAR

JANUARY • FEBRUARY

Starlings flock to roost in urban areas in the coldest months of the year. Here, it is warmer at night, as heat produced by human activities often raises the temperature by several degrees.

MARCH • APRIL

Local birds are in breeding plumage and looking for suitable places to nest, even though continental birds are only just beginning to make their return journeys to breeding grounds in eastern Europe.

MAY • JUNE

Young birds announce their presence from the nest and are noisily obvious when they fledge. First broods appear at the beginning of May, and second broods may start arriving in late June.

JULY • AUGUST

Big flocks of young birds form where there is a good food supply. The young moult gradually, losing their dull, mousy grey plumage. This is replaced by the adult feathers, which are dark and glossy.

SEPTEMBER • OCTOBER

Resident adults rarely travel long distances, but from late September to early November an influx of millions of starlings arrive, having flown to Britain to avoid the cold eastern winter.

NOVEMBER • DECEMBER

Roosting birds settle at different sites throughout the country. Roosts consist of both British birds and migrants, and tend to become bigger and fewer as the winter progresses.

Different colouring

The starling's elongated throat feathers are dark with a beautiful purple and green gloss. During the breeding season, these throat feathers are raised as the birds sing from a prominent perch. The throat feathers are longest and brightest in adult males (birds over two years old), while first-year males, most of which do not breed, sport rather less splendid feathers. There is less variation in plumage between first-year and adult females. Many females breed at a year old

but even then they are less glossy than males. Male and female birds also have different eyes – males have wholly dark eyes, but females have a pale ring around the iris, which can be hard to see.

Both males and females have yellow beaks during the breeding season. At this time, the lower mandible at the base of the beak is pink in the female but blue in the male. Resident starlings display this feature from February until June or July. Those visiting from the Continent do not develop the colour differences in their

beaks until they are ready to return to more northerly or easterly European locations in March or April.

Pair bonding

It was once believed that starlings formed monogamous pairs, with the hen laying eggs after fertilisation by the male. However, modern studies on starlings, and a variety of other birds that were originally thought to be strictly monogamous, using field observation and the latest DNA analysis techniques, have revealed a different mating pattern.

Males often attempt to mate with additional females as well as the one with which they are paired, and their advances are usually accepted. When males are absent, their female partners take the opportunity to breed with another male. In case the original mate proves to be a poor breeding choice, this gives the female a better chance of producing a healthy chick. Males, unwilling to rear a youngster that is not their own, often resort to mate-guarding in an attempt to guarantee paternity. They must be vigilant as even a momentary lapse of attention can mean that one or more eggs becomes fertilised by an interloper.

From midsummer onwards, starlings gather together in flocks. When not feeding, they often perch on wires and cables in considerable numbers. Starlings remain in the company of others until the start of the breeding season in early spring. As a consequence, the birds have often acquired their breeding plumage before group ties begin to disintegrate.

Nesting habits

Resident starlings make their nests in holes in trees – old woodpecker holes are particularly favoured – or buildings. Males choose a site and begin building their nests before searching for a mate. In courtship, the male perches near the nest, then flaps his wings and crows as females pass by. Once a pair has formed, the female usually rebuilds the nest. Starling nests are messily built from grass, leaves and, in farmland areas, straw.

Females often lay their first clutches of eggs at much the same time. They are also inclined to lay their eggs in another's nest. This is particularly common with first broods, especially where there is a shortage of nest sites. As many as a third of starling nests may contain eggs that were not laid by the incubating female. The intruder often removes one of the host's eggs from the nest, presumably making the new addition less obvious. Broken eggshells directly below the nest might alert the resident female, so the other usually disposes of the egg some distance away rather than dumping it unceremoniously over the edge. As a result, the striking blue eggs are sometimes found in gardens, on the lawn or elsewhere.

Like their parents, young starlings are noisy. They clamour loudly and constantly for food. The young lack the colourful plumage of adults, but develop this gradually over the summer months. Soon they are ready to flock to winter roosting sites.

Foraging for worms

With a distinctive, quick and confident walk, the starling forages for invertebrates, such as worms and grubs, on the ground, in open areas of short grass. Its ability to open its bill after it has pushed it into soft ground, called 'open-bill probing', enables it to collect prey from below the surface of the soil.

Roosts on radar

In the early days of radar, flocks of starlings were responsible for several false alarms. Radar was invented by the British during World War II, and the first sets detected all sorts of mysterious entities in the skies over England. These anonymous echoes were initially

▶ Clutches of young starlings usually hatch within a day or so of each other. Their parents remove the empty shells from the nest soon afterwards, and hunt for food for their demanding offspring.

▼ Long after they have left the nest, young starlings continue to return to their parents to beg them for food. Although the adults and young may be roughly the same size, their different plumage makes it easy to tell them apart.

Taking long strides, the starling struts across the ground as it eyes the soil steadily for telltale signs of movement. It may break into a run in pursuit of an escaping invertebrate.

The starling probes the ground with its sharp beak, which is supported by muscles so strong that the bird can turn over a stone if need be. It seizes worms or grubs, both for itself and its young.

BORROWED SONGS

Starlings usually sing while adopting a rather upright stance, their wings held out slightly. To sing, they perch on a branch or some other structure near their nests.

The male starling in particular is highly vocal. A bird will often return to his favourite song perch to deliver its rich, varied and often imitative songs.

While the nightingale is famous for the distinctive beauty of his song, the male starling has few British rivals for his skill as a mimic. He is able to reproduce even the most complex songs of a wide variety of other birds.

The singing skills of the starling extend to imitating the calls of tawny owls, chickens, blackbirds, swallows, and any other bird it happens to overhear. However, the starling's mimicry skills are not confined to the songs of other birds. It is regularly reported that starlings have produced wholly convincing imitations of car alarms, ringing telephones, human wolf-whistles and even whinnying horses. In this way, starlings can create some confusion.

Each male has a unique repertoire of song segments, often sung in a predictable sequence. This sequence sounds very much like an assortment of squeaks and whistles. Each bird adds new calls to its song sequence that reflect the sounds it hears around it.

Scientists disagree about the role of mimicry in starlings, but one explanation could be that the more complex a bird's vocabulary, the older and more experienced it is. To a prospective mate, maturity might be associated with a degree of fitness that has ensured the songster's survival.

form when a stone is dropped into a still pool. The point at the centre of the 'ripples' was revealed to be a starling roost, and the ripples were successive waves of starlings leaving the roost, flying off in all directions at intervals of a few minutes. The rings may be visible to an observer standing up to around 15km (10 miles) away. These flocks of birds departing the roost were returning to the feeding sites that they had found on the previous day. Roosts may even be used as

referred to as 'angels', but the true perpetrators were soon revealed to be flocks of starlings. While a single bird does not show up on a radar scan, the sheer size and density of large starling flocks meant that they generated substantial radar echoes. With the mystery solved, defence radar systems were desensitised to bird echoes.

As radar technology was improved and developed for other purposes, its potential for bird study was realised. New, amazingly consistent 'angel' patterns were observed, the most spectacular of which were seen in the mornings, just after dawn. These looked like the ripples that

A young starling begins to moult its mousy grey-brown plumage during the first autumn and winter of its life. Partially moulted birds have a patchy appearance.

'information exchange centres', so that birds unable to find good feeding sites could follow well-fed birds back to places where an abundant food supply has been discovered. The radar observations also revealed that roost catchment areas overlap, and that birds feeding in the same general area might come from two or three different roosts.

Crowded roosts

Roosting is a complex, communal activity, involving a flight display that resembles a choreographed dance. Starlings fly in tight flocks to gathering points – known as 'moots' – before flying to the roost where they perform breathtaking aerobatic displays. These are visible from many miles away, advertising the location of the roosting site to starlings that have newly arrived in Britain. In this way thousands of starlings may congregate, individuals finding safety in numbers. Although predators might be attracted to a sizable flock of birds, there is far less chance of a single bird in the flock being surprised by a hawk or falcon. In the air, the birds fly in a tight formation. Intended changes in direction are not communicated vocally but even minute shifts are translated instantly through the flock in a manner similar to the behaviour of shoaling fish.

Once within the communal roost, starlings compete for space both vertically and horizontally. Adult males take the highest and most central perches, which are not too exposed, while young females are relegated to low, peripheral sites. These are colder and more vulnerable to predators, and there is a very real hazard of being defecated upon by an upstairs neighbour. As a result of this hierarchy, each section of the roost is populated by a group of birds of the same age and sex.

◀ **A heap of windfall apples provides a feeding bonanza for a flock of starlings. Their pointed beaks are perfectly shaped for extracting the juicy flesh from the fruit.**

▼ **During the autumn and winter, starlings form flocks of thousands – sometimes tens of thousands – of birds, which habitually roost on buildings.**

WILDLIFE WATCH

Where can I see starlings?

● Although starlings have suffered a major decline over the last 30 years for reasons unknown, it is still possible to see them at dusk and to watch their aerial antics as they come in to roost in trees and on buildings. Many roosts are well-known and used every year. Late autumn and early winter is a good time to watch for them. They fly in tight flocks, performing 'synchronised flights', twisting and turning in the air. These flocks are often visible from long distances away.

● In cold autumn or winter weather, large numbers of starlings usually descend with gusto upon kitchen scraps put out in the garden. These flocks may include not only resident birds but also migrants from the more northern and eastern parts of Europe.

● In spring, at the start of the breeding season, watch for starlings as they engage in a variety of different aerial displays. The noisy flights of three or four starlings playing follow-my-leader in the sky in April and May occur as males defend their females from rivals.

● Few birds are easier to watch than starlings, as they are bold and live near humans. In spring they can be seen in their beautiful breeding plumage. Most breed in holes in trees or walls, or under roof tiles. They spend much of their time preening and advertising their presence with bursts of ecstatic song. Listen for a unique combination of warbling, chirruping, clicking and gurgling, often incorporating excellent mimicry of other birdsong and sounds.

● Although they are justifiably thought of as ubiquitous, starlings are not easily attracted into gardens or other areas that are too enclosed for the birds to feel safe. Such places may be ignored until a pair decides to breed locally and can find no other preferable nesting site. A birdfeeder in the garden might attract starlings but they will be aggressive in preventing smaller birds from approaching. They will use nestboxes but make sure that the entrance hole is large enough.

The chaffinch

Town and country gardens alike attract flocks of this elegant little bird which turns the soil for seeds and insects. Inconspicuous for the most part, the chaffinch draws attention to itself with its distinctive, trilling song.

Considered to be the second most common British breeding bird, chaffinches occupy millions of territories in Britain and Ireland. Only the wren is more numerous, although unfavourable conditions can cause the wren population to drop below that of the chaffinch.

Unsurprisingly, the largest flocks of chaffinches congregate where food is plentiful. Today, this is often in gardens where seed is provided for them, or in beech woods. Chaffinches once favoured places where corn was stored as sheaves in ricks and threshed over the winter. The waste included all sorts of seeds and chaff from the grain to which the chaffinch was partial, hence its name.

In autumn, the chaffinch becomes an even more familiar sight in gardens around Britain as around 15 million birds arrive from the colder parts of Europe, joining resident chaffinches. Most migrants come from Scandinavia but some travel from Finland and north-west Russia. Many of the birds travelling south to Britain do not fly directly across the main expanse of the North Sea, but arrive via Holland and Belgium.

A group of young chaffinches feeding on farmland in August will be made up of different individuals from a large flock foraging under beech trees in winter. The former will be the youngsters that hatched in territories near the feeding site, but the latter may include birds from several European countries as well as locals.

Life-long territory

Observations and leg-ringing records of resident chaffinches have shown that many are quite long-lived, up to 14 years, and spend their lives in more or less the same place. Some have been found within just a few hundred metres of the site where they were ringed more than ten years earlier. It seems that these birds stay on the territory they originally selected.

Through the years, and as the seasons change, these resident chaffinches accumulate much local knowledge that serves to enhance their chances of

The chaffinch picks seed from the ground in the wild. It soon becomes a regular garden visitor if it is fed, particularly after first frosts when other food may be scarce.

ALL-MALE FLOCKS

The Swedish biologist Carl Linnaeus founded the modern scientific system of naming plants and animals. In 1758, when describing the chaffinch, he noticed that the flocks remaining close to his home in winter were almost all males. As a name for this gregarious finch he therefore chose *'coelebs'*, from the Latin meaning bachelor.

There is a simple explanation for the all-male flocks noted by Linnaeus. Most chaffinches with territories in the north of Britain, or northern and eastern parts of Europe, migrate farther west for the winter. They seek out warmer areas where food on the ground will not become covered in snow. Many

Scandinavian birds come to Britain each year, but some males – particularly adults – take the risk of remaining in Sweden so that they are closer to the breeding area in spring and can have first choice of the best breeding territories. As more male than female chaffinches live in Britain in winter, it is very unusual to find a flock that includes them in equal numbers.

Linnaeus studied chaffinches on the Continent, which are slightly larger than British ones. The males also tend to have chests that are more wine-red than brick-red, but these colours are variable, and there are often exceptions to this general rule.

CHAFFINCH FACT FILE

Both male and female chaffinches of all ages are distinguished by bold white markings on the wings and white outer tail feathers. Males have deep orange-pink breast feathers. Gregarious outside the breeding season, chaffinches often form flocks, even joining other finches, such as bramblings and greenfinches.

● **NAMES**
Common name: chaffinch
Scientific name: *Fringilla coelebs*

● **HABITAT**
Gardens, parks, orchards, deciduous woodland, farmland with hedges

● **DISTRIBUTION**
Throughout British Isles; joined in winter by millions of continental visitors

● **STATUS**
Estimated at least 5,400,000 territories in Britain and 2,100,000 in Ireland

● **SIZE**
Length 14–15cm (5½–6in); weight 19–23g (¾oz)

● **KEY FEATURES**
Double white bars on wings and white outer feathers on tail, which is shallowly forked; male's face and breast are orange-pink, crown, nape and upper back grey-blue, all duller in winter; upperparts dark blackish green, grey and rich chestnut brown; female much duller

● **HABITS**
Feeds in flocks in autumn and winter; adapts to using bird tables and birdfeeders in gardens

● **VOICE**
Loud *'pink pink'* alarm note; song a rapid series of descending trills, accelerating and ending in a flourish; regional 'dialects' may be distinguished

● **FOOD**
Fallen seeds, especially beech mast, taken from ground; invertebrates, particularly caterpillars, during breeding season; windfall fruit in autumn

● **BREEDING**
Eggs laid mid-April; nest building and territorial behaviour start much earlier; replacement clutches laid until late June; occasionally 2 broods

● **NEST**
Deep cup, camouflaged with lichens and moss; generally built at head height or above, often in tree fork against trunk; failed nests dismantled and rebuilt elsewhere

● **EGGS**
Variable with pale pink, blue, grey or green background and darker red markings concentrated at broad end; 4 or 5 eggs per clutch, fewer in replacement clutches; incubation 12–13 days, by female

● **YOUNG**
Cared for by both parents for 2 weeks in nest and further 3 weeks after fledging

The female chaffinch is slightly smaller than the male, and her plumage is much less colourful – a mixture of muted greys, browns, buffs and olives.

Crown, nape and upper mantle are powdery grey-blue.

A black forehead is noticeable in the male in the breeding season.

The male's small, conical bill changes colour in the breeding season, from pinkish buff to blue-grey.

In spring, the male's plumage becomes brighter because the pale feather tips of winter wear off.

Both sexes have white edges to the tail.

Distribution map key

■ Present all year round

▨ Present during summer months

---

survival. Chaffinches that have to move away from their summer territories for the winter – including birds from northern Britain as well as from the Continent – are at a significant disadvantage in comparison. They have to search new locations for good feeding sites and often join together in large roosts of nomadic birds.

Beech trees

Where beech trees grow, the nuts – or mast – they produce can provide essential winter food for chaffinches, allowing the birds to begin the breeding season in good condition. However, beech trees do not fruit every year. In a productive season, the mast may appear in such high quantities that it seems the tree spends the next year or two recovering its vigour. Some trees produce nuts only every two or three years. Generally, though, beech trees are capable of fruiting every other year, but a poor summer and a bad autumn will result in few buds setting. Poor spring weather, particularly frost, can leave the flowers unpollinated. About twice every 10 years beech mast is fairly abundant – perhaps once in 25 years, there is a real profusion.

While beech mast is available from early autumn onwards, chaffinches can only take advantage of this bounty if they can break into the hard seed cases. Mast falling from trees in August and September on to footpaths or roads is often crushed by ramblers or cars, and the chaffinches readily take advantage of this. From October onwards, chaffinches are normally able to extract the mast themselves. A plentiful supply of mast will provide chaffinches with food until the late spring. During the summer, they feed on weed seeds from the ground, and insects.

Searching for food

While seeds form the main part of the chaffinch's diet, the birds are opportunistic feeders. While rummaging through leaf litter, they will also peck at any fallen fruit they come across, and snap up insects.

A male chaffinch hunts through the debris carpeting the ground, and is not averse to picking through any discarded kitchen scraps.

Song and plumage
The chaffinch's cheerful rattling song is one of the most familiar sounds in gardens and countryside. All year, its common call is a sharp '*pink, pink*', which punctuates the variety of sounds made by other birds visiting garden feeders.

Song is an important part of the chaffinch's courtship. It seems that the birds will not breed unless song posts are available for the cock birds. Chaffinches therefore breed in woodland, scrub, parkland, gardens and farmland hedges, but not in areas of open ground.

Chaffinches nest in hedgerows, bushes and the forks of trees. Both parents care for the four or five young, which fledge after about two weeks. When they leave the nest, the young males' plumage is duller than that of adult males but very much like that of the females. This plumage provides excellent camouflage for the young birds when they are resting or feeding, and for the female when sitting on the nest.

The male's orange-pink breast develops with the first moult in August and September. Viewed from the back or above, the male still blends in with its surroundings, despite being more striking than the female. As the brightest colours are on the underparts, they are are not visible to a cruising bird of prey. The bold blue-grey head colour is concealed by the buff tips of new feathers, and revealed again in spring.

Both males and females have gleaming white wingbars that are visible on the closed wing. In winter, chaffinches are characterised by a flurry of bold white wingbars if a flock of birds is startled from feeding on the ground. As one or two take off, the flashes of white alert the rest of the flock.

Avoiding disease
When birds flock together to feed there is always the possibility of disease breaking out. One condition that affects the chaffinch results in an unsightly growth – called a 'papilloma' – that usually occurs on the foot but may also be found on the leg. Sometimes such a growth proves fatal but it can just disappear over time.

Recent research has shown that various organisms, closely related to the pathogens that cause human food poisoning, are sometimes present in gardens. Infection causes birds to become lethargic, and they may die within a

CHAFFINCH CALENDAR

MARCH • JUNE

Local birds stake out their territories, but migrants do not leave until March or April. Breeding birds spend up to two weeks nest building. Usually a single brood is reared in May or June.

JULY • AUGUST

The young birds start to moult, making it possible to distinguish males from females. The adult birds also undergo a complete moult, shedding their worn-out breeding plumage.

SEPTEMBER • OCTOBER

Youngsters from southern areas move a short way and then settle down for life. Some northern birds migrate to warmer areas and millions of birds arrive from mainland Europe.

NOVEMBER • FEBRUARY

Large mixed flocks of British and continental birds congregate wherever food is available, especially under beech trees. If food is scarce, local birds are not joined by migrants.

The chaffinch is common in country gardens, and the birds sometimes nest in outbuildings. Double white wing bars, which are conspicuous in flight, distinguish the chaffinch from greenfinches and other small garden birds.

couple of days. Dozens of birds, not just chaffinches, may be affected as disease is transmitted by bird droppings contaminating the food. Good hygiene helps to prevent this from happening and hanging feeders are much less likely to become contaminated than bird tables or the ground. If bird food is scattered on the ground, put out small amounts so that it does not remain in the garden for several days before being eaten. Regularly disinfect bird tables and any other hard surface that is used, making sure to rinse off all cleaning substances.

As it sorts through the leaf litter, the bird discovers a dry morsel of bread, but its attention is alerted to a caterpillar, and it moves forward in short bounds.

A female chaffinch feeds her brood. Although only the female incubates the eggs, the nestlings are fed by both parents.

WILDLIFE WATCH

How can I encourage chaffinches?

● Scattering food on the ground in a safe area of the garden will usually attract chaffinches, which often become regular visitors. Unlike many garden birds, they do not become unduly aggressive when in competition for food, because they generally live in flocks and feed close together.

● The chaffinch feeds on seeds and is able to eat a wide variety of the seeds commonly included in good quality bird-seed mixtures. However, cheap mixtures often include large cereal grains that are too big for the chaffinch's beak, which is slender for a seed eater.

● Unlike birds that take seeds directly, before they drop from the plant to the ground, chaffinches do not naturally feed above ground level. They therefore need to become accustomed to feeding from a bird table and will struggle to extract seed from hanging feeders. If food appears regularly, local chaffinches will learn over several weeks or months to take food above ground level.

The chaffinch then spots the caterpillar on a leaf and, in one swift movement, grasps it eagerly in its beak. A good source of protein, any caterpillar dropping to the ground to burrow and pupate is at risk of being eaten by a hungry chaffinch.

Hoverflies

Whether glinting in the sunlight as they sip nectar from flowers, or performing astonishing aerobatic feats, hoverflies are among the most familiar of garden insects. Despite their bold warning stripes, they are quite harmless.

Most hoverflies have bands of black and yellow, like the common wasp, but they cannot sting or bite. The mimicry helps protect them from hungry birds, which are deterred by the warning colours.

Few garden flowers are without their attendant hoverflies in late summer and autumn. The domed heads of umbellifers such as angelica are especially attractive to these colourful insects, and dozens of them may be seen dining on the easily accessible nectar. They are strikingly attractive insects, with shiny, striped bodies and glittering wings, and many are excellent mimics of bees and wasps. However, it is hoverflies' agility in the air – their hovering and darting flight – that sets these insects apart from other flies. They can hover on the spot in a strong breeze, then suddenly dart away and reappear in the same place a fraction of a second later. Many species, especially the smaller ones, are completely silent in flight. Larger hoverflies, such as the belted hoverfly *Volucella zonaria*, frequently whine or buzz in flight, very like the bees and wasps that they so closely resemble.

Nectar and pollen

More than 250 hoverfly species have been recorded in Britain. They occur in almost every available habitat, from the seashore to mountain tops, although many species have definite preferences. For instance,

▼ The majority of hoverfly species have relatively short, tongue-like protuberances with which to gather nectar, and can only reach supplies that are easily accessible, such as offered by umbellifers.

A particularly impressive bee mimic, the bumblebee hoverfly, *Volucella bombylans*, has a variety of forms that each resemble a particular bee species. It is found mainly in southern Britain.

A hoverfly exuding fungus can be found clinging to a grass stem or flower head. This makes it likely that other hoverflies will come into contact with escaping fungal spores.

the scarce and striking red-belted hoverfly, *Brachypalpoides lenta*, is rarely found away from woodland, and especially beech woods. Gardens full of flowers often abound with hoverflies because of the plentiful supply of nectar. Other favoured places include woodland clearings and margins, where the variety of native vegetation supports many different species.

Adult hoverflies feed mainly on nectar, but many species also lap honeydew. Although most flies take liquid food only, some hoverflies, such as the marmalade hoverfly *Episyrphus balteatus*, are able to digest pollen grains. Pollen-feeders tend

to have short, thick probosci – tongue-like mouthparts – with broad flaps at the end, which they use to scrape up the pollen.

Unusual tastes

While adults are all flower-feeders, their larvae have remarkably varied diets. Many of them eat aphids, and are valuable pest controllers in the garden. Adult hoverflies are instinctively attracted to aphid-infested plants to lay their eggs.

As well as the aphid-eaters, there are scavengers and vegetarians. The larvae of the large narcissus fly, *Merodon equestris*, for instance, tunnel into bulbs and prevent them from flowering. Other species prefer dung, dead wood and fungi, and *Volucella* larvae feed on the dead debris in bumblebee and wasp nests. Drone fly larvae, known as rat-tailed maggots, mature in the stagnant water of ponds and ditches. They obtain oxygen through telescopic breathing tubes that extend to the surface from their tail ends.

Hoverflies have many enemies. Large numbers die in the webs of orb spiders, or are seized by lurking crab spiders. Solitary wasps stock their nests with them, and despite their close resemblance to wasps and bees, many fall prey to birds and lizards that avoid the stinging insects.

▲ Many hoverflies produce maggot-like larvae. Although the larvae have no legs, they can move surprisingly quickly. Most active by night, each one may eat more than a thousand aphids during its two-week life.

◀ The common banded hoverfly *Syrphus ribesii* is a small, active species that can be seen as late as November. Large numbers are attracted to the broad flower heads of umbellifers, such as this angelica.

Recognising garden spiders

Spiders are among the most numerous of all garden wildlife, finding plenty of opportunities to indulge their preferences for open spaces or dark corners. They employ many different tactics to trap their insect prey.

A female garden spider sits motionless, head down, at the centre of her web, waiting for a flying insect to become ensnared in the web's sticky silken spiral.

WILDLIFE WATCH

Where can I find garden spiders?

● Orb-web spiders need plenty of space to build their webs, so they are usually found in the more open parts of gardens among bushes and between tall plants, as well as on fences and across the corners of windows. The exception is the green orb-web spider, which often makes its web across curled leaves rather than across open spaces.

● The mothercare and hammock-web spiders do not need so much space for their webs, and are usually found tucked in among small trees, bushes and other tall plants. The red-and-white spider builds its scaffold web in similar places, but often nearer to the ground.

● The snake's-back spider and the window lace-weaver live in crevices and spread their webs across the surfaces of walls or trees, although the former may also be found beneath stones.

● The spotted wolf spider is a ground dweller and is most often seen when the sun is shining – either sitting waiting for passing prey or indulging in courtship display.

● Crab spiders and the nursery web spider favour lying in wait for their prey, often sitting in full view on leaves or flowers. Later in the summer the nursery web females will usually be found guarding their nursery tents.

● The zebra spider is the most active of the common garden species. When the sun is shining this small jumping spider can be seen rushing around on house and garden walls, actively seeking prey.

One delightful feature of a garden on a bright autumn morning is the way the sun glints from the dew-spangled spiders' webs that seem to festoon every branch and stem. The garden spider population often seems to have multiplied overnight, although in truth the dew has simply made their webs more visible. Many of the spiders will have been active in the garden since spring, having either overwintered as young from the previous year, or hatched from overwintered eggs. Most spiders live for less than a year.

Although the web-spinning spiders make themselves obvious, other species may be harder to find. They should be sought on plants and flowers, in crevices and beneath stones. They are also to be found hunting on the ground or, in the case of the zebra spider, running around on walls and fences.

The majority of spiders seen in the garden will be females, because the males of most species are smaller and less conspicuous. They spend much of their lives wandering in search of females. The males most frequently seen are zebra spiders and wolf spiders, which are encountered as often as females, and those of the web-building species, which often spend some time in or near the female's web before mating. Most males can be identified by larger palps – swollen growths – resembling tiny boxing gloves. These are located near the fangs,

Some spiders build elaborate webs to trap their prey, some ambush nectar-feeding insects, while others simply pursue their prey and pounce on it.

EASY GUIDE TO SPOTTING GARDEN SPIDERS

HOW CAN I IDENTIFY GARDEN SPIDERS?

● Most garden spiders are web-builders, crab spiders that lurk among flowers, or hunting and jumping spiders.

● Web-building spiders have small eyes and may be found either on their webs or in lairs adjacent to their webs. Crab spiders also have small eyes, and are crab-like in appearance.

● Spiders that hunt moving prey on plants, walls or the ground have much bigger eyes to help them line up their prey before pouncing on it. The zebra spider's two largest eyes are so big that they are larger than its brain.

● Web-builders can be grouped by their webs. The main families are orb-web spiders (Araneidae), hammock-web spiders (Linyphiidae), scaffold-web spiders (Theridiidae) and sheet-web spiders (Agelenidae). Web form is the first clue to a spider's identity.

WHAT ARE SPIDERS?

● All spiders have four pairs of walking legs and a body divided into two distinct sections – the cephalothorax and the abdomen. Most have four pairs of eyes.

● Spiders eat only live animals, which they kill by using their fangs to inject venom. The venom also helps digest their prey.

◄ The male garden spider is much smaller than his mate.

► The eggs laid in autumn will hatch in spring. The baby spiders remain together for a few days before dispersing to begin their independent lives.

GARDEN SPIDER *Araneus diadematus*

In late summer and much of autumn the orb webs of this spider may be so abundant as to fill almost every available space. The female is much more commonly seen than the male, sitting at the centre of her web with an unmistakable white cross on her abdomen. This feature gives her the alternative name of cross spider.

● SIZE
Female 10–13mm (⅜–⅝in); male 4–8mm (⅛–⅜in)

● WEB TYPE
Vertical orb web

● ADULT SEASON
Summer to late autumn

● HABITAT
Bushes, low trees, herbaceous plants, fences and glasshouses

The swollen abdomen of this garden spider indicates that she is a female.

● EGGS
Hatch in a few days, hatchlings remain within egg-sac until following spring; female remains with egg-sac until she dies, shortly after laying

● DISTRIBUTION
Abundant throughout British Isles

WALNUT ORB-WEB SPIDER *Nuctenea umbratica*

Rather sinister-looking, this somewhat flattened, black spider has a distinctly lobed, leaf-shaped marking on the abdomen. It is mainly nocturnal and is usually seen perched in its web outside windows, outlined against the night sky. Like all orb-web spiders it has eight small eyes and catches prey by sensing vibrations in its web.

● SIZE
Female 11–14mm (½–⅝in); male 8–9mm (⅜in)

● WEB TYPE
Vertical orb web

● ADULT SEASON
Females throughout the year, males summer only

● HABITAT
Trees and the outside of windows

When disturbed, the walnut orb-web will often drop to the ground on a silken line and lie motionless, as if dead, until the danger passes.

● EGGS
Female remains with eggs until she dies, within a few days of laying

● DISTRIBUTION
Common throughout Britain; scarce in Ireland

GREEN ORB-WEB SPIDER *Araniella cucurbitina*

As well as a green abdomen, this spider has a bright red spot on the underside, just above the spinnerets (glands that exude silk threads). It often spins a small web horizontally across a curled leaf, making it difficult to see against the green background, although it also spins vertical webs among green leaves.

● SIZE
Female 4–6mm (⅛–¼in); male 3.5–4mm (⅛in)

● WEB TYPE
Vertical or horizontal orb web

● ADULT SEASON
Summer and autumn

● HABITAT
Bushes and trees

The aptly named green orb-web spider is one of the most common *Araniella* species in the British Isles.

● EGGS
Female remains with eggs until she dies, within a few days of laying

● DISTRIBUTION
Common throughout Britain and Ireland

COMMON ORB-WEB SPIDER *Metellina segmentata*

As common as the garden spider, this member of the small family Tetragnathidae is somewhat slimmer and longer-legged. It varies in colour from very pale yellow through to almost red. Its web may be distinguished from those of the family Araneidae by the open space at the centre, and the way it is usually inclined at an angle.

● **SIZE**
Female 4–8mm (⅛–⅜in); male 4–6mm (⅛–¼in)

● **WEB TYPE**
Angled orb web

● **ADULT SEASON**
Late summer and autumn

● **HABITAT**
Usually near the ground

The male common orb-web spider usually waits until the female is feeding before beginning courtship.

● **EGGS**
Eggs deserted after laying

● **DISTRIBUTION**
Common in Britain but absent from most of Ireland

MISSING SECTOR ORB-WEB SPIDER *Zygiella x-notata*

A rather squat, silvery grey spider this species has a leaf-shaped mark on its abdomen. It is most easily identified by its web, which has a triangular region missing altogether – accounting for the spider's common name. These webs are often attached to window frames, but the spider hides nearby in a separate retreat.

● **SIZE**
Female 6–7mm (¼in); male 3.5–5mm (⅛–¼in)

● **WEB TYPE**
Vertical orb web

● **ADULT SEASON**
Females all year, males midsummer to autumn

● **HABITAT**
Fences and the outside of buildings

In order to remain connected to its web, this spider uses a signal thread that runs from the web centre to its lair.

● **EGGS**
Female remains with eggs until she dies, within a few days of laying

● **DISTRIBUTION**
Widespread throughout most of the British Isles; absent from parts of Scotland and Ireland

MOTHERCARE SPIDER *Theridion sisyphium*

This little scaffold-web spider has a globular abdomen with brown, reddish orange, black and white markings. It is usually to be found sitting in a tent-like lair at the top of its web, into which are woven the remains of its prey. This makes an effective, if grisly, camouflage. The name comes from the fact that the female feeds her young.

● **SIZE**
Female 3–4mm (⅛in); male 2.5–3mm (⅛in)

● **WEB TYPE**
Scaffold web

● **ADULT SEASON**
Females summer to autumn, males summer only

● **HABITAT**
Bushes, especially gorse

A female mothercare spider sits guarding her egg-sac while waiting for the baby spiders to hatch.

● **EGGS**
Female guards egg-sac until the babies hatch, then feeds them for a few days with regurgitated liquid food

● **DISTRIBUTION**
Throughout almost all of the British Isles

RED-AND-WHITE SPIDER *Enoplognatha ovata*

Closely related to the previous species, this yellowish white spider usually has distinctive red markings on its globular abdomen – either a single red band down the centre, or two distinct red bands. In some individuals these bands may be broken up to form rows of spots. In others, they are absent altogether.

● **SIZE**
Female 4–6mm (⅛–¼in); male 3–5mm (⅛–¼in)

● **WEB TYPE**
Scaffold web

● **ADULT SEASON**
Summer

● **HABITAT**
Bushes and other low plants

The red-and-white spider has a very potent venom that can quickly immobilise prey as big as a bumblebee.

● **EGGS**
Female sits beneath a leaf guarding the egg-sac until hatchlings emerge

● **DISTRIBUTION**
Common throughout almost all of the British Isles

HAMMOCK-WEB SPIDER *Linyphia triangularis*

Belonging to the family collectively known as 'money spiders', the hammock-web spider is one of the largest of the group. It has a shiny dark brown abdomen marked with whitish or yellowish streaks, and is usually to be found hanging upside down beneath its slightly domed, horizontal web. These webs are very numerous in autumn.

● **SIZE**
Both sexes 5–6mm (¼in)

● **WEB TYPE**
Scaffold above a hammock

● **ADULT SEASON**
Midsummer to late autumn

● **HABITAT**
Bushes, small trees and other vegetation

A female hammock-web spider feeds on a bug that has become trapped in her dense, complex web.

● **EGGS**
Female remains with eggs until they hatch, shortly after laying

● **DISTRIBUTION**
One of the most common spiders in the British Isles

WINDOW LACE-WEAVER *Amaurobius fenestralis*

This lace-web spider, a member of the family Amaurobiidae, has a dark brown carapace – a hard shield that protects its thorax – and a velvety black abdomen, with a central cream stripe through which runs a dark line. Typically, these spiders produce ribbons of fluffy, non-sticky silk, which they use to spin sheet-webs.

● **SIZE**
Female 7–9mm (¼–⅜in); male 4–7mm (⅛–¼in)

● **WEB TYPE**
Untidy mesh across a wall or fence with central retreat

● **ADULT SEASON**
Females all year, males summer only

● **HABITAT**
Walls, stones and logs with crevices in which to form lairs

The web of a lace-weaver is woven flat against a surface. A hole in the web's centre leads to the spider's retreat.

● **EGGS**
Laid in disc-shaped silk sac in silk-lined burrow; female stays with young for around 4 months after they hatch

● **DISTRIBUTION**
Widely distributed in Britain, less so in Ireland

SNAKE'S-BACK SPIDER *Segestria senoculata*

A tube-web spider of the family Segestriidae, the snake's-back has a dark brown, almost black carapace and a noticeably long, tubular grey-brown abdomen. A row of darker marks along the top of its abdomen resemble the dark zig-zag markings of an adder. This slim spider has six eyes instead of eight, and big, powerful jaws.

● **SIZE**
Female 7–10mm (¼–⅜in); male 6–9mm (¼–⅜in)

● **WEB TYPE**
Silk tube in a hole from which radiate silken threads

● **ADULT SEASON**
Spring to autumn

● **HABITAT**
Crevices under stones, in bark and in walls

The snake's-back spider usually stays hidden in its lair until an insect blunders into one of its tripwires.

● **EGGS**
Laid in holes in walls and the bark of trees and shrubs; female usually remains until the young disperse

● **DISTRIBUTION**
Common throughout the British Isles

ZEBRA SPIDER *Salticus scenicus*

The only really common jumping spider (family Salticidae) found in gardens, the zebra spider has distinctive black-and-white stripes. The male has long, forward-pointing black jaws, but the most noticeable features are big eyes that the spiders use to target their insect prey before pouncing on it and killing it.

● **SIZE**
Female 5–7mm (¼in); male 5–6mm (¼in)

● **WEB TYPE**
None

● **ADULT SEASON**
Summer

● **HABITAT**
House and garden walls and fences

A zebra spider will often sit back and take a close look at whoever is observing it, with big, jet black eyes.

● **EGGS**
Laid in egg-sacs in silken cells; female guards them until hatchlings emerge around a month later

● **DISTRIBUTION**
Throughout England

SPOTTED WOLF SPIDER *Pardosa amentata*

This drab hunting spider of the family Lycosidae has a dark carapace with a paler central line, and a brown abdomen with rows of darker spots. Males signal to females with their black palps (sensory appendages) to indicate that they wish to mate, and this behaviour can often be seen on sunny days in summer.

● **SIZE**
Female 5.5–8mm (¼–⅜in); male 5–6.5mm (¼in)

● **WEB TYPE**
None

● **ADULT SEASON**
Females spring to autumn, males to midsummer only

● **HABITAT**
The ground

The female is most conspicuous when carrying a pale egg-sac attached to her spinnerets (silk glands).

● **EGGS**
Female carries egg-sac with her, helps the babies emerge, then carries them on her back for several days

● **DISTRIBUTION**
Very common throughout almost all of the British Isles

NURSERY WEB SPIDER *Pisaura mirabilis*

Elegant and sleek, this spider is grey to brown with a much paler stripe down the centre of the carapace. The abdomen is paler along the sides, and along the top is a variable leaf-shaped mark. The nursery web spider is a member of the family Pisauridae, and one of just three European species.

● **SIZE**
Female 12–15mm (½–⅝in); male 10–12mm (⅜–½in)

● **WEB TYPE**
None, apart from nursery tent

● **ADULT SEASON**
Summer

● **HABITAT**
Low vegetation, especially nettle beds

The nursery web spider is a relatively large, but slender hunting spider, with a habit of basking in the summer sunshine.

● **EGGS**
Female carries egg-sac slung beneath her body, held by her fangs; spins a silken tent in which the babies hatch, and guards this for up to a week or so until the young disperse

● **DISTRIBUTION**
Common in England and Wales, less so in Scotland and absent from northern parts of Ireland

COMMON CRAB SPIDER *Xysticus cristatus*

This is the commonest of the crab spiders (family Thomisidae), which seize prey in their powerful front legs. The female varies from very pale to dark brown, but usually has a dark, backward-facing triangular mark on the carapace and a pattern of triangles on the abdomen. The darker, smaller male is likely to be seen only when courting the female.

● **SIZE**
Female 6–8mm (¼–⅜in); male 3–5mm (⅛–¼in)

● **WEB TYPE**
None

● **ADULT SEASON**
Spring to early summer

● **HABITAT**
Low bushes and shrubs, stone walls and also the ground

A female crab spider feeds on a leaf weevil that has strayed close enough for her to pounce upon it.

● **EGGS**
Laid in egg-sac in silken tent built on a leaf; female guards this until hatchlings emerge

● **DISTRIBUTION**
Widely distributed throughout the British Isles

WANDERING SPIDER *Philodromus aureolus*

Although similar to the common crab spider, this reddish brown species has longer legs and no carapace triangle. Unlike other crab spiders, which sit in wait for prey in likely spots such as flowers, this species hunts actively and is likely to be seen scuttling over plants looking for its insect food.

● **SIZE**
Female 5–6mm (¼in); male 4mm (⅛in)

● **WEB TYPE**
None

● **ADULT SEASON**
Spring and summer

● **HABITAT**
Bushes and low trees

While sitting motionless, lying in wait for passing prey, the wandering spider can be quite difficult to spot.

● **EGGS**
Female guards egg-sac, often sitting in full view on top of a leaf

● **DISTRIBUTION**
Common in England and Wales; patchy in Scotland and Ireland

Garden fungi

Sometimes overnight the damp grass of a lawn becomes speckled with fungi, forming rings or gathering in clusters. They perform an important function in recycling organic matter to make the soil more fertile.

Fairy-ring champignon

In the British Isles over 100 species of fungi form circles, or fairy rings, but *Marasmius oreades* is the best known, as indicated by its common name. On its own, one of these toadstools is unremarkable, with a pale buff cap up to 5cm (2in) across, widely spaced, cream to buff gills and a tough, dry, pale brown stem. However, it rarely grows on its own. Fairy rings appear on lawns from spring to autumn, usually after rain, and although some gardeners may find them unsightly, they have no long-term detrimental effect on the grass, merely causing some discoloration.

The development of a fairy ring can be observed over the years. Starting off as a small circle, the ring gets bigger each season as the mass of fungal threads spreads out underground, although each toadstool lasts for a few days at most. A zone of dark grass indicates the size of the ring, with the toadstools appearing on its rim.

▶ The grass inside the circle may be in poor condition, choked by the threads in the soil, but at the centre of larger circles, as the fungi die, the grass recovers.

WHAT ARE FUNGI?

Fungi comprise an entire kingdom of biological organisms. They lack the green pigment, chlorophyll, that plants use to manufacture food by photosynthesis. Instead, they obtain energy by breaking down organic matter, as animals do. Most feed on decaying material, but some species also attack living tissue.

The main part of any fungal organism consists of fine threads called hyphae. These form a network – or mycelium – beneath the surface of the soil or in dead or dying vegetation. This persists and grows for decades, and is responsible for turning decaying material into food.

The mushroom or toadstool that appears above ground is the short-lived fruiting body of the mycelium. It is formed from tightly woven hyphae and its function is to produce and release spores. This is usually achieved via gills, pores or other structures on the fruiting body, which is raised above ground on a stalk to assist the spores' wind dispersal.

In the case of bracket fungi, the fruiting bodies often sprout directly from the place where the mycelium is growing, such as a decaying tree stump.

Psilocybe crobulus

A close inspection of the lawn in September may reveal a delicate little fungus straggling up through the grass, its stems topped with tiny, flesh-coloured caps. If the margin of each cap is fringed with what resemble miniature teeth – in fact, the remains of the veil that once enclosed it – then the species in question is likely to be *Psilocybe crobulus*.

This fungus favours areas of damp ground and usually grows in small clusters. It is inedible and possibly mildly toxic, but given its small size it is unlikely to be considered for consumption anyway.

Psilocybe crobulus seldom grows taller than the grass stems among which it grows. It is usually necessary to part the vegetation to get a good look at the whole fungus.

Yellow stainer

Although similar to the edible field mushroom, and a close relative, this large species is definitely one to avoid because it can cause severe stomach upsets if it is eaten. A common species, it sometimes grows in gardens and parks, and can usually be identified by a number of distinctive characteristics. For instance, the white cap is up to 15cm (6in) across, and when young it stains bright yellow when bruised – as does the cut flesh at the base of the stem. The flesh itself has a distinctly unpleasant inky or chemical smell. Furthermore, the ring on the stem is larger and more persistent than in most of its relatives.

◀ Look for the yellow stainer in the short grass of lawns, on bare soil and bark mulches, and among dead leaves. It can appear at any time from late summer right through the autumn, although it is most likely to be seen on days following heavy rain.

Parrot wax-cap

In autumn the lawns of many mature gardens are likely to be dotted with small, brightly coloured fungi, sporting roughly conical, shiny caps with an almost greasy texture. These belong to a large group of fungi called the wax-caps.

The parrot wax-cap is one of the most widespread and distinctive of this family. If they are growing in a group, it soon becomes apparent that each individual specimen is a subtly different mixture of colours, because the precise hue of parrot wax-caps varies according to their age. Young fungi are bluish green, but they become reddish and orange with age and finally yellow.

▲ The shiny appearance of the parrot wax-cap is most noticeable in damp weather or after rain. This fungus often grows among mosses.

▶ Also known as the 'magic mushroom', the liberty cap is a common grassland species in late summer and autumn, especially in September.

MUSHROOM DEVELOPMENT

Large fungi, such as field mushrooms, often appear in gardens and parks literally overnight. Their fruiting bodies are adapted for rapid growth, the cap and gills changing colour as spores are produced and released, often within just a few days.

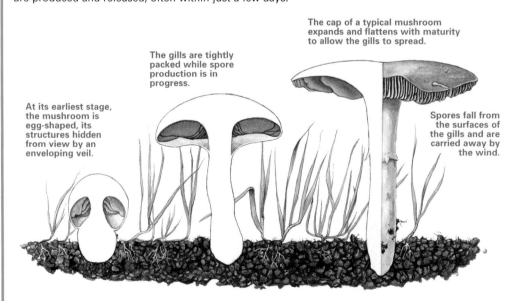

The cap of a typical mushroom expands and flattens with maturity to allow the gills to spread.

The gills are tightly packed while spore production is in progress.

At its earliest stage, the mushroom is egg-shaped, its structures hidden from view by an enveloping veil.

Spores fall from the surfaces of the gills and are carried away by the wind.

Liberty cap

The presence of this delicate fungus is no threat to the lawn or garden, but it is notorious for other reasons. If eaten in sufficient quantity, it is known to produce hallucinogenic effects, and processing it in any way is illegal.

There are several similar small fungi to be found on the lawn in September, but the liberty cap is easily recognised by the pointed tip of its domed cap and, often, a blue-green stem base. The cap is pale olive-grey when fresh and moist, becoming buff-cream as it dries out. The gills darken with age from grey to violet-brown as the spores ripen.

Parasol mushroom

This edible mushroom sometimes appears on lawns in mature gardens from late summer, especially where the grass has been left undisturbed for some time. The cap, which can reach a diameter of 30cm (12in) or more when fully expanded, is pale grey-brown, but is covered in darker shaggy scales. The stem is also scaly and has a double ring. The gills are white or cream.

Unlike some fungi, the parasol does not pose any threat to the garden or the lawn. The grass where it grows seems to fare just as well as in areas where it is absent.

▶ The cap of the parasol mushroom is club-shaped or domed and rounded at first. As the spores ripen on the gills, the cap expands and flattens, broadening out to give the appearance of a wide, flat parasol.

Rickenella fibula

There can be few more delicate garden fungi than this one. Its long, slender stems are little broader than those of the grasses that it grows among, and its cap is only 5–10mm (just under ½in) across. Its appearance has earned it the nickname 'carpet pin fungus'.

Rickenella fibula favours damp, mossy parts of the lawn, where it appears in summer and autumn. The thin cap is usually pale orange, while the gills and stem are pale yellow. The species poses no threat to the garden, although its presence is often a sign that the ground beneath is waterlogged.

◀ Radiating dark lines on the cap's upper surface give *Rickenella fibula* a fanciful resemblance to a half-opened oriental parasol. The fungus is easily damaged by mowing.

Honey fungus

The very mention of this species is enough to cause knowledgable gardeners to shudder, since honey fungus has a well-deserved reputation for killing garden trees and shrubs. Most clumps are likely to be associated with trees that are already dead. However, by means of long, shoelace-like mycelial strands, honey fungus can locate and attack living trees as well, eventually causing a terminal rot.

Honey fungus can be recognised by its orange-tan cap, which is flecked with dark scales. The gills are yellowish buff and the stem, which bears a ring, is brown with darker scaling towards the rather bulbous base.

▼ Honey fungus has honey-coloured caps that are speckled with brown scales, concentrated mostly in the centre. The fungus forms dense clumps where it is well established.

Brown roll-rim

As well as being one of the most abundant woodland fungi, this species is also common in gardens and parks in late summer and autumn. One necessary condition for its growth, however, is the presence of trees – particularly silver birches – since the underground mycelium of the fungus lives in association with the tree roots, and the two supply each other with nutrients. This alliance between fungus and tree appears to be benign, so the appearance of brown roll-rim fungi beneath garden birch trees is no cause for concern. However, it is very poisonous to humans.

Dull yellowish brown at first, the brown roll-rim becomes more hazel brown with age. The caps of young specimens have inrolled margins, but as they mature they often expand and flatten, sometimes becoming concave.

Many-zoned polypore

Leaving the stump of a dead tree in place, or constructing a log pile in a quiet corner of the garden, can create a perfect habitat for many types of garden wildlife that feed on dead timber.

Freshly felled timber is often too hard for many of these creatures, but a sure sign that it has aged nicely is the appearance of fungi such as the many-zoned polypore. This aptly named bracket fungus is abundant on old wood all year round, and is an attractive addition to the garden in its own right.

◄ **The upper surface of the many-zoned polypore is covered in concentric rings of different, and very variable, colours. The under surface is peppered with pores through which the white spores are released.**

Field mushroom

This much-prized edible mushroom is often common on lawns, where it poses no threat to the garden. Despite its size – the cap can reach a diameter of 10cm (4in) – the field mushroom can easily be overlooked in grass that has not been mowed for some time.

The whitish cap of the field mushroom has a silky texture. The stem is also white with a delicate, fibrous ring that is easily lost. When young, the gills are dark pink, but as the spores ripen the gills become chocolate brown, darkening still further with age. Unlike some of its close relatives, the field mushroom has a pleasant smell – the classic scent of mushrooms.

► **Field mushrooms can appear on the lawn at any time from midsummer to late autumn, usually following prolonged rainfall. This is a mature specimen, with a broad cap and dark brown gills.**

WILDLIFE WATCH

Should I encourage fungi in the garden?

● Most garden fungi should be regarded as allies. They work hard to break down organic debris, helping to add nutrients to the soil. However, an exception to this rule is the parasitic honey fungus, which attacks trees and can be a serious problem. If the soil is infected with honey fungus, it is difficult to grow anything in it.

● In order to encourage beneficial species that speed up the recycling of organic matter, consider using wood chippings on herbaceous borders as a mulch. Remember, however, not to use it anywhere near mature trees, owing to the remote possibility that the wood chippings may contain honey fungus spores.

● Avoid mowing some areas of the grass during peak toadstool fruiting time, which occurs from early September until the middle of October. This allows the fungi growing on the lawn to shed their spores before they die back.

Shaggy ink-cap

One of the easiest garden fungi to identify, the shaggy ink-cap is instantly recognisable at all stages of its development. It is also edible, but only young ones are really worth eating. In any case, few people would consider the blackened older specimens.

It appears from late summer and throughout autumn. It first appears as an egg-shaped structure, which is actually the closed-up cap. Its shape is quite unlike that of the mature fungus, but its surface is covered with shaggy scales. Over a period of a day or so the closed cap rises from the ground on a robust, bulbous-based stalk. As it ripens, the gills and lower edge of the cap blacken and gradually dissolve into an inky fluid, which contains the spores.

Also known as the 'judge's wig', the shaggy ink-cap is unmistakable. The scales on the margins of the cap are usually the first part of the fungus to break down.

Ragworts and groundsels

The brightly coloured flowers of these familiar plants – often seen in gardens as well as growing wild – cheer up town and countryside throughout the year. They spread by means of feathery 'parachutes' or barbed fruits.

The yellow, daisy-like flowers of the ragworts and groundsels indicate that these plants belong to the family Asteraceae, which includes daisies, dandelions and thistles, among many others. This family used to be known as the Compositae and the family members are still often referred to as 'composites'. The leaves of ragworts and groundsels are usually cut into lobes and are deeply toothed. The related gallant-soldier and bur-marigolds have opposite pairs of toothed leaves.

Another relative, leopard's-bane, has heart-shaped, toothed leaves.

The flowers, which are grouped in loose or dense clusters near the top of the stems, are composed of many small florets. The base of each flower is anchored in a bowl-shaped receptacle surrounded by a circle – or involucre – of green, sepal-like bracts.

Ragworts and groundsels have two types of floret – disk-florets and ray-florets. The ray-florets radiate outwards, like petals, while the mass of tiny disk-florets combine to form the flower's centre. Each disk-floret consists of five petals fused into a tube. This is encircled by fine white hairs, which are greatly reduced sepals. In ragworts this ring of hairs – called a pappus – is feathery while in groundsels the hairs are stiff bristles.

Five male stamens and a female stigma enable each floret to produce a single seed, although in this family, the structures known loosely as seeds are actually tiny, one-seeded fruits. Once the fruits have formed and the flower has withered, each pappus acts like a parachute to disperse the fruits on the wind.

In bur-marigolds, the disk-florets are usually contained by yellow-brown bracts rather than ray-florets and the outer, green bracts curve away from the flower head. The fruits have tiny barbs and are distributed by hooking on to the fur of passing animals.

Widely scattered

Ragworts, groundsels and their relatives include annual, biennial and perennial species that are hardy and adaptable. Most prefer open, previously dug or marshy ground. Some cultivated or introduced species, such as silver ragwort, Oxford ragwort, gallant-soldier and leopard's-bane, have escaped from gardens and colonised surrounding areas.

Groundsel, on the other hand, often invades gardens. It may be welcomed by rabbit and canary owners because it can be fed to these animals, but not by gardeners because it takes root in flowerbeds and vegetable patches. The name groundsel comes from the Anglo-Saxon word *grondeswyle*, which means 'ground swallower'. Not only do these plants grow quickly, but their seeds can lie dormant in the soil for several years.

Ragwort control

Common ragwort is a handsome plant, but it must not be allowed to grow in pastures grazed by cattle and horses. Livestock find the plant unpalatable and tend to avoid it, but if the plant is cut for weed control or as part of a hay crop, the animals may inadvertently eat it and be poisoned. The cocktail of toxic alkaloids contained in ragwort causes liver damage over a period of months and is often fatal. For this reason, the law states that landowners must remove any ragwort from their land in case it invades neighbouring properties.

The golden flowers of common ragwort persist well into the autumn, creating a colourful display on waste ground and sometimes even river banks.

DID YOU KNOW?

Caterpillars of the cinnabar moth feed voraciously on the leaves of common ragwort even though they are toxic. The caterpillars store the toxins in their bodies, making them poisonous to predators. Their black and yellow stripes are a warning to leave them alone.

RAGWORT FACT FILE

● Common ragwort
Senecio jacobaea
Habitat and distribution
Abundant on dry, overgrazed pastures, roadsides, woodland margins, waste ground and sand dunes
Size 30–150cm (1–5ft) tall
Key features
A biennial or short-lived perennial with erect, tough, leafy stems branched in upper part; leaves compound, deeply dissected and toothed, hairy beneath, end tooth short and blunt; flower heads yellow, 15–25mm (⅝–1in) across, in dense, flat-topped clusters, 12–15 rays
Flowering time
June–November

● Marsh ragwort
Senecio aquaticus
Habitat and distribution
Common on damp grassland, marshes, river banks and ditches
Size 30–80cm (1–2ft 8in) tall
Key features
Similar to common ragwort but biennial, with lower stems loosely branched; leaves less dissected, shinier, end lobes large; flower heads 25–40mm (1–1½in) across, in looser, broader clusters
Flowering time
July–August

● Hoary ragwort
Senecio erucifolius
Habitat and distribution
Common in places on dry, rough grassland and waysides on clay or lime-rich soils in England and Wales; in Ireland only in County Dublin and extreme south-west
Size 30–120cm (1–4ft) tall
Key features
Similar to common ragwort, but a more greyish, hairy, clump-forming perennial, with branches lower down and short runners; leaves paler, with deeper, narrower pointed lobes; flowers paler yellow, 12–20mm (½–¾in) across
Flowering time
August–October

● Silver ragwort
Senecio cineraria
Habitat and distribution
Escapes from gardens occur on dry banks, sea cliffs and shingle beaches, especially in southern England, Wales and County Dublin
Size 30–60cm (1–2ft) tall
Key features
A low-growing, silvery, woolly perennial, with tough, branched, leafy stems that are woody at the base; leaves compound, deeply dissected and bluntly toothed; flower heads yellow, 8–20mm (⅜–¾in) across, in dense, rather flat-topped clusters
Flowering time
June–August

● Oxford ragwort
Senecio squalidus
Habitat and distribution
An escape from Oxford Botanic Garden in 1794, now common in cities, towns and suburbs, on railway ballast, walls, waste ground and road verges; rare in Scotland, mostly in larger cities in Ireland
Size 20–50cm (8–20in) tall
Key features
A branched, almost hairless annual, biennial or short-lived perennial; leaves compound, deeply dissected; flower heads bright yellow, 16–20mm (¾in) across, in loose, irregular clusters, 12–15 rays, 8–10mm (⅜in) long; bracts around flower head conspicuously black-tipped
Flowering time
April–November, sometimes December

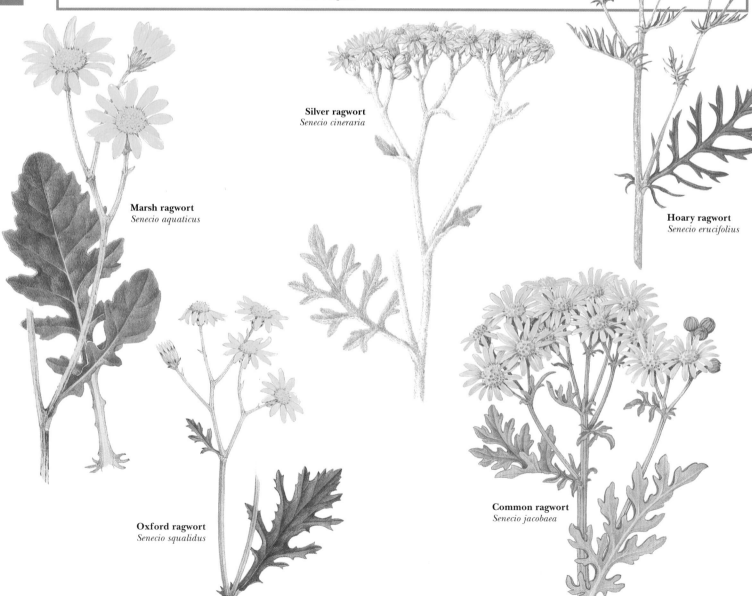

Marsh ragwort
Senecio aquaticus

Silver ragwort
Senecio cineraria

Hoary ragwort
Senecio erucifolius

Oxford ragwort
Senecio squalidus

Common ragwort
Senecio jacobaea

GROUNDSEL FACT FILE

● **Groundsel**
Senecio vulgaris
Habitat and distribution
Abundant on disturbed land and waste ground, especially in spring and autumn
Size 10–30cm (4–12in) tall, sometimes taller
Key features
An erect, branched, often cobwebby, hairy annual; leaves coarsely and bluntly lobed; flower heads yellow, 4–5mm (⅛–¼in) across, in irregular clusters, rays usually absent; tiny bracts around flower head conspicuously black tipped
Flowering time
January–December

● **Sticky groundsel or stinking groundsel**
Senecio viscosus
Habitat and distribution
Widespread but local on railway ballast, waste ground, roadsides and shingle beaches; scarce in Ireland
Size 20–60cm (8in–2ft) tall
Key features
A bushy, densely sticky-hairy, foetid annual; leaves dark green, coarsely, bluntly lobed and toothed; flower heads yellow, 6–12mm (¼–½in) across, in branched clusters, rays 6–8mm (¼–⅜in) long, soon rolling downwards
Flowering time
June–October

● **Heath groundsel**
Senecio sylvaticus
Habitat and distribution
Heaths, woodland margins and disturbed ground on sandy and gravelly soils
Size 20–70cm (8in–2ft 4in) tall
Key features
An erect annual, with often rather sticky, downy, branched stems; leaves yellowish green and irregularly lobed; flower heads yellow, 4–6mm (⅛–¼in) across, in flat-topped clusters, rays short, soon rolling downwards, bracts purple tipped
Flowering time
June–September

Groundsel
Senecio vulgaris

Heath groundsel
Senecio sylvaticus

Sticky groundsel or stinking groundsel
Senecio viscosus

Originally a native of southern Europe, Oxford ragwort gained its misleadingly English-sounding name when specimens from the Oxford Botanic Garden were sent to the famous Swedish naturalist Carl Linnaeus for a formal description.

RELATED PLANTS FACT FILE

● **Gallant-soldier**
Galinsoga parviflora
Habitat and distribution
Introduced from Peru and now
patchily common on previously dug
or cultivated ground, especially in
London and south-eastern England
Size 10–50cm (4–20in) tall,
sometimes up to 80cm (2ft 8in)
Key features
An erect, branched, almost hairless
annual; leaves in opposite pairs,
oval, toothed, narrowing up the
stem; flower heads 3–5mm (⅛–¼in)
across, disk-florets yellow, with
scales along them, 3-lobed; 4–6
rays, short, white; fruits black,
flattened, each with tuft of scales
Flowering time
May–November

● **Shaggy soldier or hairy
soldier** (*Galinsoga quadriradiata)* is
similar but has stems covered with
long, spreading white hairs and
unlobed or scarcely lobed scales in
the disk; most common in London.

● **Leopard's-bane**
Doronicum pardalianches
Habitat and distribution
Naturalised from gardens in
woodlands and shady places,
especially in eastern Scotland
Size 30–100cm (1–3ft 4in) tall
Key features
An erect perennial, forming
patches; basal and lower stem
leaves heart-shaped, toothed,
stalked; upper leaves spear-
shaped, clasping stem; flower
heads yellow, 30–45mm (1¼–1¾in)
across, in small, branched clusters,
rays about 25mm (1in) long; bracts
around flower head in 2 ranks
Flowering time
May–July

● **Trifid bur-marigold**
Bidens tripartita
Habitat and distribution
Widespread and locally abundant
on margins or drying mud of rivers,
lakes, ponds and ditches; absent
from most of Scotland and Ireland
Size 30–60cm (1–2ft) tall
Key features
A branched annual with winged,
purplish stems; leaves in opposite
pairs, 3 or 5-lobed with a pair of
lobes at the base, coarsely
toothed; flower heads yellow,
15–25mm (⅝–1in) across, in very
loose, branched, leafy clusters;
rays usually absent
Flowering time
July–October

● **Nodding bur-marigold**
Bidens cernua
Habitat and distribution
Widespread but somewhat less
common than trifid bur-marigold, in
similar habitats
Size 30–70cm (1ft–2ft 4in) tall
Key features
Similar to trifid bur-marigold but
more robust; leaves narrowly
spear-shaped; flowers larger,
nodding; yellow rays rarely present
except in north-west England
Flowering time
July–September

Gallant-soldier
Galinsoga parviflora

Leopard's-bane
*Doronicum
pardalianches*

Nodding bur-marigold
Bidens cernua

Trifid bur-marigold
Bidens tripartita

WILDLIFE WATCH

Where can I see ragworts, groundsels and their relatives?

● Ragworts favour old pastures,
disturbed ground, woodland
margins, roadsides, river banks and
even sand dunes.

● Groundsels grow on light or
disturbed soils and on waste ground.
Sticky and heath groundsels also
grow on roadsides and woodland
margins.

● Gallant-soldier, and its more local
relative shaggy (or hairy) soldier,
often grows in gardens, nurseries
and allotments. Look for leopard's-
bane in woods and plantations,
especially in Scotland. Both species
of bur-marigolds occur on drying
mud and watersides.

Native trees in the garden

As flowering plants die down in late summer, many native trees are reaching their full autumnal glory. Branches ablaze with vividly coloured leaves and eye-catching berries, carefully chosen species can enliven even compact gardens.

In every season, trees provide a framework in the garden but in autumn, as flowers wither and die, they become valuable focal points, often displaying colourful foliage and distinctive berries. Nut or fruit-producing native trees also have the advantage of enticing a variety of birds and small mammals into the garden to feed.

In urban areas, outdoor space is often fairly restricted. For those people with town gardens, who fear that tree roots will damage the foundations of their houses, a native tree with a modest spread of branches is a good choice, providing it will thrive in the aspect and soil conditions of the intended site.

Colourful trees

The slender elegance of the native rowan – or mountain ash – is ideally suited to the smaller garden. This tree grows best in an open, unshaded location that gets plenty of sunshine, and it prefers peaty soils with good drainage.

Covered in white flowers in late spring or early summer, by autumn its foliage turns fiery shades of orange and yellow. In this season its clusters of berries turn orange or red as they ripen. These attract blackbirds and thrushes as well as winter-visiting fieldfares and redwings. As an alternative, the variety known as 'Joseph Rock' has unusual yellow berries.

The common alder is a medium-sized tree that needs more space than the rowan. Its cone-like fruits change gradually from soft green to woody brown as they ripen. The winged seeds they contain are eaten by waxwings, tits and finches among other birds. In late winter and early spring, the tree is draped in drooping male catkins. In the wild, common alder is often found along the banks of streams and rivers.

Modest in size, the crab apple looks attractive for most of the year. In autumn, it is laden with brightly coloured fruits – suitable for making jams – which tempt a wide variety of birds into the garden. Earlier in the year, in April or May, its branches are festooned with flowers, which range from white tinged with pale colour to shades of red, depending upon the variety. Bred more than 100 years ago, 'John Downie' is one of the best cultivated crab apple trees. It has white flowers and tapering orange and red fruits.

▲ Rowan's sparse foliage allows grass to grow beneath it. From midsummer, clusters of orange, red or yellow berries appear.

◀ With its glorious spring blossom and colourful autumn fruits, the crab apple is a popular choice for the garden. It grows best in full sun, in rich loam soils with good drainage.

▶ The leaves of the common alder turn golden yellow in autumn. The tree thrives in sunny, damp conditions.

Tolerant trees

Like the crab apple, whitebeam is popular in town gardens because it tolerates restricted space and moderate air pollution. It even copes with dry, exposed sites. Whitebeam has striking looks for most of the year but especially during autumn, when its foliage becomes golden and it produces masses of pillar-box red berries.

The foliage is also an appealing feature of the tree in spring. The young leaves are densely covered beneath with downy white hairs, giving the tree a silvery-white appearance, from which its common name is derived. Even before the creamy white flowers appear later in spring, whitebeam can look as if it is in bloom. As the leaves of whitebeam grow over the course of the summer, they lose their hair and appear duller, but this is soon compensated for by the vibrant autumn foliage.

For a nut-producing native tree that will attract wildlife, hazel is useful as it thrives in either shade or full sun. If left to grow naturally, it forms a multi-stemmed tree. Hazel has been cultivated for more than 4000 years because its straightest branches

▲ The compact shape and modest size of whitebeam have made it a popular garden tree. In May, it is adorned with creamy white, sweetly scented flowers.

have many uses, including basket making. Two of the most attractive hazels are 'Aurea', which has golden foliage, and the decorative corkscrew hazel, 'Contorta', the strongly twisted branches of which are much more evident when the leaves have fallen.

Silver birch is a popular choice for urban gardens because of its hardy nature, its small size and the fact that it grows quickly. Although it prefers a sunny position in well-drained soil, it will nevertheless grow well in exposed areas.

In autumn, the leaves of the silver birch change from pale green to golden yellow, falling to carpet the ground beneath the tree. In winter, its magnificent silver trunk is visible through pendulous leafless branches. Many insects lay their eggs in the soft timber of elderly silver birch trees, and the grubs that hatch provide food for woodpeckers.

Cultivated varieties suitable for the garden include Young's weeping birch 'Youngii' and the purplish maroon-leaved 'Purpurea'.

▲ Hazel produces nuts that are popular with squirrels, dormice and wood mice, as well as urban pigeons and jays. It can be planted to form a dense, living boundary to the garden.

Light, delicate foliage and a silvery white trunk make the silver birch an attractive addition to any garden. Throughout autumn and winter, the tree retains a striking appearance.

WILDLIFE WATCH

How do I grow native trees from seed?

● Native trees are easy and fun to grow, for adults and children alike. Collect seeds in autumn then sow them into a potted mixture of half grit and half soil. Place the pot in the garden in a light but sheltered position. Covering the pot with wire netting is the best way of preventing rodents from stealing the seeds.

● Most types of tree should germinate the following spring, but be patient as some require two winters to break their dormancy. After they have germinated, pot the plants individually and, in early summer, transfer them to their final locations. Remember to water them well during their first summer.

Park watch

- The brown rat
- The family life of feral cats
- The treecreeper
- The woodpigeon and stock dove
- The nuthatch
- Recognising slugs
- Weevils
- The crane-fly

- Willowherbs
- Recognising small trees and shrubs

The brown rat

Intelligent and adaptable, the brown rat flourishes by waterways, in parks and in built-up areas. It finds plenty of food and shelter with the help of its sensitive whiskers, acute hearing and sharp nose.

For a rodent that arrived in the British Isles fewer than three hundred years ago, the brown rat has settled extraordinarily well. Its original homeland lies in Central Asia, where it bred in immense numbers before spreading westwards in the 18th century. It soon established colonies across the Continent, and probably reached Britain by being accidentally imported from Russia in ships' cargoes. This adaptable creature soon replaced the long-established ship or black rat as the most common rat species in these islands.

Carelessly stored food, thrown-out scraps and feed scattered for chickens offered them plenty to eat in both town and country but they became most firmly established in city drains and sewers. Food was constantly available and they used these hideaways as strongholds. In the 19th century, as public health became a political issue and the railways expanded to create large conurbations, the sewer system was also extended, providing convenient routes for dispersal. Eventually, rats arrived in Scotland, where they were slow to colonise some of the remoter areas, where fewer people lived.

There are now millions of brown rats in Britain. According to the Government-endorsed National Rodent Survey of 2003, the brown rat population has reached 60 million – which means that the British Isles is home to more rats than people.

Living together

Brown rats live in colonies, which may be founded by a single pregnant female or by a small group of animals moving in together. The place in which they choose to settle depends to a great extent on the availability of food but their extremely varied diet gives them a huge number of alternatives. Those that do not live in drains or buildings or on farms, often live by water.

The brown rat appreciates areas with thick cover near water and will often venture along the banks of park lakes in search of the nests of waterbirds. As a result it is sometimes mistaken for a water vole. The rat, however, has a more pointed nose.

BROWN RAT FACT FILE

As well as being able to swim well, the brown rat can climb and leap with great agility, using its chunky tail as a balance. On the ground, it trots along fairly fast, but slows down, often swaying from side to side, while foraging.

● **NAMES**
Common names: brown rat, common rat, Norway rat
Scientific name: *Rattus norvegicus*

● **HABITAT**
Often inside buildings; in hedgerows, rubbish dumps – anywhere with a source of food

● **DISTRIBUTION**
Throughout mainland Britain including city centres and most offshore islands

● **SIZE**
Length head and body up to 29cm (11⅛in), tail three-quarters length of body; ear 2cm (¾in); very variable, males generally larger; weight usually about 275–520g (9¾–18¼oz), occasionally up to 800g (28oz)

● **STATUS**
Common, possibly 60 million individuals

● **KEY FEATURES**
Large, heavily built with coarse, shaggy fur, greyish brown to black above and paler grey on underparts; ears small, finely haired; tail thick, scaly, often appears pinkish or pale grey

● **HABITS**
Wary; predominantly nocturnal, with peaks of activity generally a couple of hours after sunset and a similar time before sunrise; lives in colonies

● **VOICE**
Shrieking squeak or piping or whistling (males) when alarmed or attacked; communicates by ultrasound (inaudible to humans)

● **FOOD**
Virtually anything, from seeds to soap; fruits, stored foods and meat; will kill other small birds, insects, mice and other small mammals; steals eggs

● **BREEDING**
Throughout year, usually producing 7–9 young per litter

● **NEST**
In burrows, sometimes under debris; made of grass, shredded paper or other soft material; may change site every 1–2 weeks

● **YOUNG**
Leave nest at about 3 weeks old, weighing about 40g (1⅜oz); uniformly pale grey all over; often mistaken for an extra-large mouse

● **SIGNS**
Small, black oval droppings, averaging about 15–20mm (⅝–¾in); gnawed wood, paper or other material

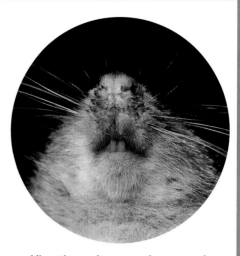

Like other rodents, rats have two sharp front teeth in both the upper and lower jaws. These are naturally coloured yellow and are used to gnaw food and many other items, including lead pipes.

Distribution map key

▉ Present all year round

☐ Not present

Long blackish hairs form a coarse, shaggy-looking coat. Underlying it is softer underfur.

Thick and scaly, the tail is less than the length of the body.

Prominent ears are pinkish with fine fur.

Delicate fingers on the forepaws can manipulate food, while sharp claws enable rats to climb well.

Rats' trails

Brown rats are quick to learn about their environment and establish well-defined runways. To compensate for their poor eyesight, they have a highly developed 'kinesthetic sense', which means that they memorise their surroundings and navigate around familiar objects even when they have been removed.

Using its excellent sense of smell, the rat sniffs out the odour trails left by other rats. These scents not only enable the rat to learn that another animal has passed recently, but also to recognise kin.

The rat scurries along unobtrusively. This industrious rodent and its relatives will have established many trails and tunnels in the area.

Warily, the rat checks for dangerous scents, even at the risk of a fall, confident that its supple body will absorb the impact.

The brown rat spends a considerable part of its time licking and grooming its fur and whiskers. Living in fairly dense colonies means good hygiene is important.

In urban areas, many canals, park lakes and ponds attract colonies of rats because these places provide a good living for the rodents all year round. In general, rats prefer grain, but they also eat fresh vegetables, meat, bones and may even turn cannibal if they are short of food. In parks, they can plunder the detritus left by humans and supplement this with any dead fish they find in the lakes. In spring and summer, they are particularly fond of birds' eggs. As well as game birds' and hens' eggs, moorhens' eggs are among their favourites, but they will take any waterfowl eggs and sometimes even attack the young birds.

Larger morsels of food are often carried off to be eaten in the safety of the burrow or somewhere out of sight, where stores may be kept in case of future need. They also take shiny objects out of curiosity and soft materials for nests.

Groups of brown rats may even live along parts of the coast, where they feed on rock-pool fish and shrimps exposed at low tide, and raid seabird nests in summer. They will eat dead birds and eggs, as well as the numerous insects and sandhoppers found on grassy cliffs and dunes.

Brown rats can swim from the time they are eight days old, although they have no special physical adaptations for taking to water. They stretch out their front legs and paddle with each hind leg alternately. Being able to swim for hours, providing the water is not too cold, and remain underwater for a couple of minutes, helps them to avoid predators rather than to hunt for prey.

Social structures

Colonies vary in size from a few to several hundred. Large colonies tend to be dominated by big, high-ranking males and their associated females, who take up residence in the best places, which are those closest to food.

Rats can travel considerable distances, sometimes more than 3km (2 miles) in a single night. This enables them to colonise distant places, taking advantage of new areas and sources of food, if necessary. However, once settled, rats normally stay in the same area, within 50m (165ft) or so of their regular food supply.

In farmland, rats travel around half a kilometre (a third of a mile) in a night, scurrying along a hedge and out into neighbouring crops. Often the same pathways are used repeatedly, and the distinct trails created may be followed for some distance from the colony's burrows.

In summer, rats living on farms often colonise hedges, spreading into open countryside. This appears to be a less favourable habitat than the environs of human habitation, though, and the population often dies out or moves on during the winter.

Able to detect faint glimmers, the rat is on the lookout for light. It is incapable of bringing objects into clear focus. Rats are also almost certainly colour blind.

When the rat reaches an obstacle, its short, heavy tail helps it to balance as it leaps nimbly upwards. The tail also helps when the rat scurries along narrow ledges.

Keen senses

Rats use scent to enable them to find their way about and also to learn where other rats have been. Their sense of smell is extremely well developed and their hearing is acute, but their vision is relatively poor. Rats are mainly active at night, just before sunrise and after sunset, but will also come out during daylight, especially if the nights are very cold.

Like other rodents, rats have a single pair of front teeth – incisors – which they use for gnawing. They have no canine teeth – just three molars in the upper and lower jaw on each side, used for grinding – and the space behind the incisors can be closed with folds of skin so that the rat does not have to swallow everything it gnaws. In fact, they constantly gnaw any suitable material to prevent the incisors from growing too long. Sometimes they choose soft items such as candles and bars of soap, but they also gnaw wood. The gnawing can be dangerous. If they choose to hone their teeth on the insulation around electrical cables, for instance, it can lead to short circuits and even fires. They will also gnaw lead pipes, causing leaks.

Careful grooming

Normally, rats groom their fur meticulously, first licking their front paws and using them to wash head and ears and then progressing to stomach and sides. They use their hind feet only to scratch and, if necessary, will nip at any parasites, such as fleas and mites, with their incisor teeth.

However, grooming may be neglected in dense colonies, and the animals become dirty and scruffy. Moreover, the filthy places where some feed, in sewers for example, mean that their fur becomes contaminated with harmful bacteria. These are then carried into the food stores visited by rats. This role as a carrier of disease is the main hazard to public health posed by rats.

The brown rat is also a carrier of Weil's disease, which can be fatal to humans. This is caused by bacteria called leptospires, which live in the kidneys and are excreted in the urine. The leptospires can remain infectious in damp places for long periods. They are mainly a danger to

▲ A female with young will defend them against most visitors. However, if the nest is disturbed, she will often carry them to a safer place. If she feels too threatened to attempt a rescue, she may resort to cannibalism.

▶ Baby rats are born after a pregnancy lasting slightly more than three weeks. The babies are weaned after 20–23 days and the mother typically has another litter almost straightaway.

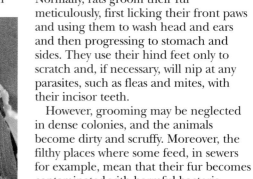

▲ A rat finds the nests of gamebirds such as pheasants and partridges an easy source of eggs to eat, especially where these are located on the ground under the hedgerow where it lives. Gamekeepers regard a rat as a major pest.

people who work in wet areas frequented by rats, such as sewer workers and farm workers. Most other people are unlikely ever to encounter the disease.

Natural aggression
A brown rat will sometimes attack if cornered by a mammalian predator, such as a cat. Turning to face its attacker and remaining motionless until the cat moves, the rat will suddenly lunge forward with loud squeals and teeth bared.

Rats are also aggressive towards their own kind, especially in overcrowded colonies or where food is scarce. Strange rats will be inspected carefully by sniffing, then challenged. Often two rats will rear up on their hind legs and have a boxing match, clawing at each other. When one breaks off to run away, the other gives chase and bites its rump. This is why subordinate animals in colonies often have little fur left on their back, and show many bite wounds on their rump and around the base of the tail.

Burrows and nests
Among their many other abilities, rats can dig well and they usually excavate their own burrows, using their front feet and teeth. They kick loose debris away with the hind feet but turn round to push most of the soil out of the tunnel.

▲ Generally, a rat prefers starchy food, such as grains, although it will eat just about anything, even other rats. This varied diet is an important factor contributing to the success of the species.

The burrows are fairly complex with separate chambers for living and storing food, and side passages in which to hide and deposit droppings. There are often several entrances and the burrow system of one colony may sometimes connect with the excavations of another.

The nest is built in the living area and the rat never spoils it with urine or faeces but keeps it clean. Just about any available material is used to construct the nest, from grass and leaves to paper, electricity cable and insect remains. Everything is brought in by mouth and piled in a heap. When the weather is cold, the rat carefully builds it into a cosy nest. It does not work on its nest in warm weather.

▼ Traditionally, a rat is thought to be a threat to food stores on farms and in warehouses. However, most storage units have now been made resistant to rats and mice.

Sometimes rats will take over and adapt disused rabbit burrows. In parks, they burrow into lakesides or river banks and on farmland, they build their nests in any available straw or hay, preferably in barns.

Breeding machines
Rats living in colonies that are based under cover, with plenty of food nearby, can breed continuously, with a third of

INGENIOUS RATS

Rats are skilled problem solvers, far superior in this respect to other small mammals. A number of reports suggest that rats may assist each other to their mutual benefit. For example, two rats are reported to have cooperated to get a piece of biscuit through the bars of a cage. In several cases, rats are said to have assisted each other in stealing eggs from chicken coops.

They also use their ingenuity in transporting eggs to their food store, overcoming man-made obstacles. One report from Devon tells how a rat clasped an egg under one front leg and proceeded to climb up and over a vertical wall using just the other three.

White rats are derived from albinos, which are naturally tame. Bred through many generations, they become extremely docile. These animals can make attractive pets and will reveal their natural intelligence by learning to perform tricks for rewards of food.

Tunnels and mazes are often used to study rat behaviour, allowing the mammal to display its intelligence and adaptability.

females pregnant at any one time during the year. Outdoors, breeding is seasonal. Larger females have larger families. Occasionally, as many as 11 young may be born, but the average litter is seven to nine. Pregnancy lasts for just over three weeks and the babies are born blind and helpless. Their eyes open at six days and they are weaned at around three weeks. Females can breed at 11 weeks and may produce five litters in a year. By the time a female is having her third litter of the year, those born in her first litter will already be breeding.

By late summer, therefore, the population can build up very quickly. This is balanced by heavy mortality – fewer than 10 per cent of rats live more than a year. In fact, most die young, when they are inexperienced and more vulnerable to predators. Most of the rats taken by

▲ Exceedingly agile, the brown rat can climb fast, even up vertical brick walls, using its claws to grip the rough surface. These animals can also leap a metre (3ft) straight up and nearly two metres (6ft) in a long jump.

▲ Water is no barrier to the brown rat, which can stay afloat for up to 72 hours. It is able to swim the length of several football fields in order to cross rivers and reach islands, where its impact on nesting birds is often devastating.

owls weigh less than 100g (3½oz). Weasels, stoats and cats also eat many of these little rats, which are usually less than three months old. However, after the rats reach about 200g (7oz) they are too big to cope with easily. Adult rats defend themselves ferociously if attacked, although otters and mink are not deterred. In urban areas, especially parks, foxes are the rat's main predator, although the major threat is probably motor cars. The brown rat is one of the most common victims of road traffic in Britain today.

Wary rodents

Brown rats continue to thrive partly because they can cope with a great variety of natural conditions, including extreme cold, but also because they are very suspicious of unfamiliar objects in their home areas. Consequently, they are reluctant to enter traps. They will avoid new objects for several days, and perhaps never go near them.

Brown rats are not often fooled by poisoned baits laid down outside traps. Even if a rat does approach and start to nibble the poisoned food, it will not usually eat enough to be fatal and, as a result, may even begin to develop immunity. Some rats have begun to acquire a genetically inherited resistance to the most widely used modern rat poison, Warfarin.

WILDLIFE WATCH

Where can I see brown rats?

● Park lakes and ponds are good places to watch for brown rats. Municipal rubbish tips are another good bet. Although operators try to ensure that their sites are free of rats, it is extremely difficult to get rid of all of them.

● Canals, or the ditches and hedges around a sewage works (especially if a small, old-fashioned system is in operation) are places where the chances of seeing rats are high.

● Farms, mills and other places where spilt grain is likely to be in evidence would be good to visit. Chicken sheds are often ideal sites, although the owners will do their best to ensure that rats are few or absent.

◀ A rat is capable of communication using ultrasonic sound waves. These are used to signal distress or pain, and also in play and in courting the opposite sex.

The family life of feral cats

Although living wild, feral cats often rely on humans for food, especially if rats, mice and small birds are hard to find. They have a long breeding season, so kittens and young cats are often part of a group all year round.

Cats are the most abundant carnivorous mammal in Britain. There are around nine million in all – one million living wild and eight million domestic cats. The larger an animal is, the more it must eat to survive. At an average weight of at least 3kg (6½lb) each, cats add up to a greater tonnage than all other British carnivorous mammals put together. Many cats, including domestic ones, live at least partially wild, preying on birds and mammals – sometimes with a severe impact on local populations.

Domestic cats that have reverted to living completely wild are described as feral. These are lost or abandoned pets and their descendants. The availability of

food usually limits animal numbers, but in towns humans often put out meals for feral cats as regularly as every night. This ensures the survival of more cats than might otherwise be the case. As a result, there is frequently a greater concentration of feral cats in urban areas than in the countryside.

In towns and cities, feral cats inhabit old factory sites, dockyards and the grounds of hospitals, as well as parks, churchyards and wasteland. In some places, there are more than 10 feral cats per hectare (2½ acres). These cats are not tame, but take cover by day in bushes and old buildings, emerging at night to scavenge anywhere there might be scraps

▼ To give birth to her kittens, a female seeks a safe, secluded spot – in urban areas, this may be a quiet wooded glade in a park. The family stays together until the kittens can fend for themselves at three months old.

▶ Each kitten must practise the skills it needs to hunt prey. Birds form part of the feral cat's diet, so the kitten needs to be able to climb trees. It uses its sharp, retractable claws to grip on to branches.

A feral cat can be aggressive towards another, especially to an intruder on its territory. When threatened, it snarls, hisses and spits, baring its sharp teeth and perhaps flexing its claws. However, serious fights between cats are rare.

DOMESTIC CATS AND PREY

Even domestic cats catch a vast quantity of wild prey in a year – probably an average of at least a dozen victims each. In one year, the 70 cats living in one Bedfordshire village killed at least 1090 small birds of 22 different species. This total included about one third of all the young house sparrows in the village. Generally, town cats kill more birds, but mammals – mostly voles and wood mice – make up about two-thirds of the prey of country cats. Prey may be eaten or taken home as presents for the cats' owners.

Even 10-year-old cats can be adept at catching mice, although younger ones are usually more successful. Among the more surprising cat prey are lizards, newts, toads and frogs – as well as the declining populations of harvest mice, slow-worms and young grass snakes.

Wearing a bell may reduce the numbers of mammals that a domestic cat can catch by ambush. Most wild mammals are nocturnal so that keeping cats indoors for the night prevents them from roaming around at the same time as their prey. Bad weather has the same effect, because cats are less successful at hunting in windy and wet conditions, and more inclined to stay indoors.

▲ Practising hunting skills, such as stalking and swift pouncing, is natural behaviour – whether a domestic cat is hungry or well fed.

◄ Many areas of parks, cemeteries and urban wasteland develop long, lush grass to which cats, domestic or feral, retreat when they want to lie up during the day or stalk small birds and mammals such as mice.

of food and to feed on what local cat-lovers have left out for them. Many feral cats depend on this food, especially as autumn turns to winter. Then hunting conditions worsen as the weather becomes harsher and prey scarcer. At this time feral cats are likely to be seen at dusk, or heard at night as they forage in dustbins or raid bird tables.

In the country, many feral cats live around farmyards, stalking the birds, rats and other small mammals that inhabit barns and outbuildings. Truly feral cats live completely independently of humans. On some offshore islands they survive by preying on seabirds and rabbits.

Matriarchal society
Feral cats usually live in small groups of about 10 animals. Each group consists of a female cat and several generations of offspring – mostly daughters, with females in the group outnumbering males by about three to two. The group lives together amicably, sharing the same territory but driving out other cats. One dominant female is often the main breeding animal – subordinate females rarely produce young at all. Male feral cats roam widely, visiting several groups of females. Young males often remain in the female-dominated group into which they were born until they are about two years old, before challenging established mature males for supremacy. Some youngsters may lose such battles and be driven away to live alone.

When a feral cat meets another of its own group, the cats may raise their tails in greeting and rub heads and flanks. Cats have scent glands under their chins, on

the top of their heads, along the midline of their backs and along their tails, so this behaviour transfers scent and reinforces group identity. During the day, when feral cats rest, related individuals may sleep side by side, which also serves to strengthen social bonds.

Characteristic behaviour
Feral cats may follow tracks made by larger animals, such as badgers, but prefer to use their own network of paths. They prowl along hedgerows and fences, stalking baby rabbits, birds and mice. In country areas, cats roam widely when

Some cats are good 'ratters' and keep down the numbers of rats that inhabit gardens and farm buildings. A small rat like this is enough to feed a cat for a day, although it will kill more if the opportunity arises.

WILD CAT COUSINS

Complete body stripes distinguish the wild cat from the tabby feral cat, which is blotched. The wild cat also has a more rounded tail, whereas the tabby has a pointed tail, like other feral cats.

Feral cats pose a threat to the recovery of the wild cat population that is currently confined mainly to Scotland. As the wild cat moves into new areas, it comes into increasing contact with the feral cat. The two can interbreed and produce fertile offspring, which means that, with time, the genetic purity of the wild cat could become diluted. Feral cats and wild cats often live side by side, and hybrids are nearly impossible to distinguish from true wild cats – particularly as the cats are usually glimpsed only briefly and in the dark. Sightings of 'lookalikes' may even have contributed to the apparent spread of the wild cat into new parts of Britain in recent years.

The usual definition of a species is a group of animals that can interbreed to produce fertile offspring. Hybrids between wild and feral, or domestic, cats are fertile, which implies that both parents were the same species. If this is so, then the legal protection given to the wild cat is hard to define – either all cats have to be protected or none. It has been proposed that wild cats and hybrids 'of wild cat appearance' should be protected – a ruling that means domestic tabby cats could be covered as well.

A car breaker's yard makes an ideal home for feral cats. The old vehicles are rarely moved and provide numerous dark lairs in which to hide. They also offer protection from the weather and human disturbance.

hunting, females often over 10 hectares (25 acres), while males may cover an area as large as a square kilometre (just under half a square mile). In towns and cities, feral cats rarely travel far. Remaining close to their dens, they often live their entire lives within an area of less than a tenth of a hectare (a quarter of an acre).

Although they are active mainly at night, feral cats come out during the day to bask in the sun. Kittens usually spend long periods playing, which prepares them for catching prey and engaging in territorial battles with other cats. Particularly during moulting, the cats spend a lot of time grooming their fur, licking themselves all over with their rough tongues. Like domestic cats, feral cats moult twice a year, in spring and autumn. In autumn they acquire thicker fur to help them cope with the cold winter months. In spring this is replaced by a lighter summer coat.

Cats dislike getting their paws wet and generally avoid patches of mud and pools of water. This means that feral cats rarely leave paw prints, unless they happen to walk on very soft ground. Then the prints have a characteristic round pad with four round toes. Their claws do not leave an impression because they are retracted when the cat is walking.

To mark their territories, feral cats spray urine backwards against a wall or other upright object. Males do this more often than females, and their urine is pungent. Droppings may also be left as scent markers, although within the territory – and especially near buildings – many cats attempt to bury them. These droppings

usually contain masses of fur or feathers from prey and can look very like those of foxes. However, cats have relatively weak jaws, so bone fragments are rare in their droppings. By contrast, fox droppings often contain large lumps of shattered bone, broken by the fox's powerful jaws.

Secluded den

Feral cats make dens in outbuildings, wood piles and haystacks – any dark and secluded space in which they can hide during the day. In these safe havens, the breeding female gives birth to up to three litters each year. Most young are born between January and August, although cats may breed all year round in some urban areas. The number of times that a female breeds depends on her condition and how much food there is available.

Many feral cats depend on scraps put out by humans. However, in urban areas a feral cat will also forage for food among rubbish, including half-emptied packets and tins.

▲ A feral cat that has become unafraid of humans may sit on a car bonnet that has been warmed by the sun or by the heat of the engine. On cold days, a feral cat may even crawl into the engine cavity.

◄ A disused building offers safe shelter to a feral cat. It prefers to live near humans, especially in urban areas where more of its food comes from scavenging than from hunting.

Pregnancy lasts for two months, and the kittens are blind and helpless at birth. It takes two weeks for their eyes to open, three weeks before they can stand up and two months to grow a full set of teeth. The kittens feed on their mother's milk while they develop, and become independent when they are about three months old. At this time their eyes change colour from milky blue to greenish yellow.

The feral cat population may be augmented by abandoned pets that seek to join a colony. The newcomers are often attacked by resident tom-cats and are likely to have trouble finding sufficient food in their new and unfriendly world.

On farms, feral cats may be useful, hunting pests such as rats and mice, but in towns they can be a nuisance, scenting posts with their pungent urine and wailing loudly in the night.

When feral cats breed freely, the increase in numbers causes diseases such as cat flu to be transmitted more readily. Those animals in poor condition, through lack of food for instance, are particularly susceptible and many of them may have difficulty in breathing and some die. To counter this, some animal welfare organisations, including the RSPCA, often have programmes to catch feral cats and neuter them. They then release the animals back into their territories, which prevents more cats from moving in to replace them.

Feral cats come in all shapes and sizes and can be difficult to distinguish from domestic cats. A mixture of tortoiseshell and tabby, such as these two, is one of the most usual colour forms, but pure black and black with white markings are also fairly common.

WILDLIFE WATCH

Where can I find feral cats?

● By torchlight at night, explore the quiet streets and open spaces behind restaurants, railway stations and hospital grounds – particularly in areas where food may have been left. Small parks and cemeteries may also be home to groups of feral cats. It's best to visit secluded places in a group, but remember to approach quietly. Listen for the loud wails of tom-cats, especially in the spring.

● Cats are usually nocturnal, but those that live in towns and are fed in urban parks and gardens have little to fear from humans and they may appear in daylight. On sunny days they may be seen lounging on rooftops and walls, wherever there are warm spots.

● An organisation that deals specifically with feral cats is the Original Cat Action Trust. Contact them at 11 Lower Barn Road, Purley, Surrey CR8 1HY or visit www.catactiontrust.org.uk

● Other animal welfare organisations concerned with feral cats include Cats Protection (CP) and the RSPCA. For information, contact Cats Protection at the National Cat Centre, Chelwood Gate, Haywards Heath, West Sussex RH17 7TT (telephone 08707 708649) or visit www.cats.org.uk Contact the RSPCA at Wilberforce Way, Southwater, Horsham, West Sussex RH13 9RS (telephone 0870 33 35 999) or visit www.rspca.org.uk

The treecreeper

This little bird is constantly on the move, flitting from tree to tree in search of food. Brown streaky plumage on its back allows it to blend in with its surroundings when danger threatens.

Silence falls over British parks and woodlands in autumn. Some areas may seem to be devoid of songbirds, but the birds are still there. Most small songbirds stop singing at this time of year and some form flocks that travel around in search of the best places to feed. If disturbed, a roving flock will suddenly bring the trees to life, with small birds flitting between the branches, feeding furiously and calling softly to each other to ensure that the group keeps together. These roaming flocks are made up mainly of members of the tit family but they are often joined by other species, including treecreepers and goldcrests.

Treecreepers are never still. This small brown bird moves restlessly up – never down – the trunk, typically spiralling round the tree so that one minute the bird is in view and the next it has disappeared. Once the treecreeper has reached the top – or about 16m (50ft) up a tall tree – it will fly down to the base of a neighbouring tree and repeat its spiralling ascent in search of food. The treecreeper's jerky, shuffling movement is characteristic, as it presses its tail against the wood for support, all the while investigating the trunk for insects and their larvae.

Tree dweller

The treecreeper is perfectly suited to life in parks and woods. It seeks its food in the bark of tree trunks and on the undersides of larger branches. Its longish, delicate, down-curved bill is superbly adapted for probing crevices and its long, curved claws enable it to hang from the undersides of branches with ease. Brown plumage with buff and blackish markings helps to give the treecreeper excellent camouflage against the bark, especially in the dappled sunshine that pierces the woodland canopy. It also has a silvery white breast, but if threatened, it will press itself against the trunk to disguise this feature.

Like woodpeckers, treecreepers have strong, stiff tail feathers, which they use as a prop when climbing. These feathers are so important that treecreepers, along with woodpeckers, have a different pattern of annual moult from most other small

When the treecreeper takes flight, the pale banding along its wings becomes clearly visible. The bird is much harder to spot when it is climbing up a tree trunk.

DID YOU KNOW?

In 1979 in Lancashire, a pair of treecreepers were found incubating a clutch of eggs that included a single blue tit egg. A few days later, the baby blue tit had hatched and was being reared by the treecreepers. Young blue tits take longer to fledge than treecreepers, but these devoted foster parents continued to feed the young blue tit even after their own young had left the nest. Eventually, the adopted blue tit fledged successfully.

TREECREEPER FACT FILE

During its short, somewhat undulating flight, the treecreeper's silvery underparts and pale wing bands are much in evidence. Its long tail, which is divided into two points at the end, also stands out clearly.

● **NAMES**
Common names: treecreeper, common treecreeper, Eurasian treecreeper
Scientific name: *Certhia familiaris*

● **HABITAT**
Deciduous, coniferous and mixed woodland; parkland and gardens with mature trees

● **DISTRIBUTION**
Throughout most of Britain and Ireland

● **SIZE**
Length 12.5cm (4¾in); weight 9g (¼oz)

● **STATUS**
Estimated 200,000 territories in Britain and 40,000 in Ireland

● **KEY FEATURES**
Brown with pale streaks; white underparts; buff wingbar; ragged pale stripe over eye; long bill, curving down slightly; long, stiff, pointed tail feathers

● **HABITS**
Climbs tree trunks and branches in series of short hops; spirals up one tree and then flies to the base of a nearby tree and starts again

● **VOICE**
Thin, high-pitched *'tsee, tsee'* call; can be hard to hear; song high-pitched trill followed by a higher-pitched warble that can also be hard for humans to hear

● **FOOD**
Insects, especially stoneflies, beetles, crickets, earwigs, lacewings, caterpillars and spiders; some small seeds in winter, especially pine or spruce

● **BREEDING**
Egg laying starts in early April, peaks late April and early May; 1, occasionally 2, broods per season

● **NEST**
Built in cavity, often behind flaking bark on tree trunk; nest cup woven on top of small sticks and pine needles

● **EGGS**
3–9 (usually 5 or 6) white, finely speckled eggs; female incubates for 14 days

● **YOUNG**
Fed by both parents; leave nest after 15 days; independent about 7 days later

The longish, slender bill curves downwards.

Long, sharp claws give a good grip.

A white eyestripe stretches along the head.

Brown upperparts are mottled with paler and darker bars and patches.

Stiff, pointed feathers end the long, brown tail.

Distribution map key

Present all year round

Not present

birds. The long central tail feathers are retained until all the other feathers have regrown.

High-pitched song
Territories are established in February and March and are generally well spaced. At this time, and on into April, the treecreeper's song is most commonly heard, although it is high-pitched and at the edge of the range of the human ear. It is heard again for a short time in autumn. The male sings from a variety of song posts within his territory. He may also sing in flight as he defines the area in which he and his mate will nest and feed. Rival males meeting on a territorial boundary become highly agitated, performing 'song duels' and flicking their wings. If these displays do not resolve the dispute, the birds may fight, flying up together with their claws locked, before fluttering back down to the ground.

The treecreeper will build its nest behind flaking bark on a tree or cladding on a building, in a slit in a tree trunk or hole in brickwork, or in some other suitable cavity. In some parts of Europe these birds are known to use the same site for many years, but in Britain it seems the treecreeper varies the location of its nest each time.

The male selects a range of alternative sites and marks them with small pieces of nest material. The female will choose one and build her nest in it within about a week. She partly fills the cavity with small twigs, pine needles and dead leaves. On top of this sturdy foundation she builds a

TREECREEPER CALENDAR

JANUARY ● MARCH

In winter, treecreepers join roving feeding flocks of tits and other small birds as they move around the woodland or venture out into hedgerows. As spring approaches, they start to establish breeding territories.

APRIL ● JUNE

The female builds her nest in a tree hole or a hollow behind flaking bark. Usually five or six eggs are laid and the young hatch about two weeks later. They huddle together while they wait for food.

JULY ● SEPTEMBER

Young treecreepers and adults moult their feathers. Some start to sing again for a time in autumn. Both adults and juveniles leave their territories and join mixed roving flocks.

OCTOBER ● DECEMBER

At night, treecreepers huddle into roosting cavities, such as hollows made in the bark of giant redwoods. With their feathers fluffed up for warmth, they are beautifully camouflaged against the tree trunk.

A tiny crevice in the bark of a wellingtonia or redwood tree is a favourite roosting site for a treecreeper. These introduced trees are doubtless popular because the soft, fibrous bark is easy to excavate and is insulating.

A nest that is located behind loose bark is often so narrow that when incubating the eggs or brooding the nestlings, the female treecreeper cannot even turn round. Such a tight fit keeps out predators effectively.

delicate nest cup, made of moss, spiders' webs, fine grasses, hair, feathers and other soft materials.

The male provides his mate with food from the time nest building begins until the eggs hatch. This 'courtship feeding' has two benefits – it provides the female with extra food during the critical period of egg laying and incubation, and also cements the bond between the pair. The female incubates the clutch of five or six eggs for about 14 days. She also broods the young, but they are fed by both adults and can fly after about 15 days.

Huddling together

After leaving the nest, young treecreepers continue to be fed by their parents for another week before they become independent. During this time, they stay close together, both during the day and at night. Some pairs, especially those breeding in conifer woods, will raise a second brood, which often overlaps with

the first – a new nest may be constructed and even eggs laid before the first brood has fledged.

Generally, treecreeper families and pairs split up for the autumn and winter, although some birds will remain together. It is at this time that the treecreepers roam beyond their territories with parties of tits and other small birds. British treecreepers rarely travel far – few individuals journey more than 5km (3 miles) from their nest sites, although they may venture out of parks and woods to visit thick hedges with trees.

Travelling with other birds has real benefits. Scientists have shown that the rate of feeding increases when treecreepers mingle with mixed flocks. The level of safety that is achieved by so many pairs of eyes looking out for predators means that more time can be spent searching for food. This is critical during the limited hours of daylight in winter, when birds have to find enough nourishment to give them the energy to survive the long, cold nights.

At night, treecreepers roost in crevices in tree trunks or hollows that they have excavated themselves. Some trees, notably

▲ In the limited confines of the treecreeper's nest, it is important to keep the young clean. Therefore, the adults collect the chicks' droppings – neatly encapsulated in faecal sacs – and carry them off to dispose of them.

Onward and upward

The treecreeper has a systematic approach to hunting. Like an animated flake of bark, it progresses up a tree in a series of spasmodic jerks – unhurried but never still, turning round and round the trunk and under branches in a corkscrew spiral.

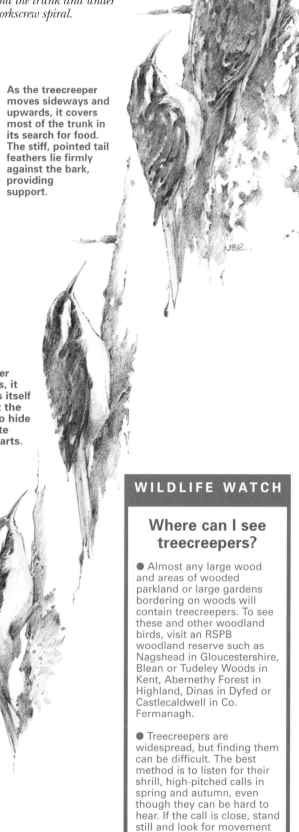

As the treecreeper moves sideways and upwards, it covers most of the trunk in its search for food. The stiff, pointed tail feathers lie firmly against the bark, providing support.

If danger appears, it presses itself against the trunk to hide its white underparts.

The treecreeper clings to the trunk, intently listening to locate beetle larvae and other prey.

Starting from the base, the treecreeper shuffles its way up the trunk using its sharp claws and strong legs.

redwoods – or *Sequoias* – are popular and often contain several roost sites. Wellingtonias, which are commonly found in mature parks and gardens, are even more favoured. Roost holes are oval-shaped depressions in the bark and those that are in regular use can be easily recognised by the distinctive white droppings that collect on the bark below the hollows.

Close relative
In mainland Europe, the treecreeper is usually found in coniferous forests. Lowland deciduous woodlands are inhabited by the closely related short-toed treecreeper. This bird can be reliably distinguished from the treecreeper only by its voice. Even then, although some of their calls are distinct, each species may mimic the other's song. Indeed, these two birds are the most difficult of all European birds to distinguish from each other. However, in Britain the short-toed treecreeper breeds only in the Channel Islands, where the treecreeper is absent.

Fluctuating population
When woodland covered much of Britain some 5000 years ago, treecreepers were probably very numerous. As forests and woods were cleared, numbers may have declined but the treecreeper was able to adapt to living in parkland and among conifers and hedgerows with trees.

The main cause of several sharp declines in numbers over the last hundred years has been particularly severe winters, such as the one that occurred in 1978–9. Along with many other small birds that feed primarily on insects, treecreepers suffer high mortality when their food is locked away in a glaze of ice. Today, with less harsh weather and despite the ancient woodland being fragmented, the treecreeper population appears to be stable.

WILDLIFE WATCH

Where can I see treecreepers?

● Almost any large wood and areas of wooded parkland or large gardens bordering on woods will contain treecreepers. To see these and other woodland birds, visit an RSPB woodland reserve such as Nagshead in Gloucestershire, Blean or Tudeley Woods in Kent, Abernethy Forest in Highland, Dinas in Dyfed or Castlecaldwell in Co. Fermanagh.

● Treecreepers are widespread, but finding them can be difficult. The best method is to listen for their shrill, high-pitched calls in spring and autumn, even though they can be hard to hear. If the call is close, stand still and look for movement on a nearby tree trunk. In autumn and winter, look for the roost holes in redwoods and Wellingtonias.

The woodpigeon and stock dove

The soft, muffled cooing of a plump woodpigeon is an increasingly familiar sound in parks and gardens, sometimes complemented by the gruff, resonant call of its smaller cousin, the stock dove.

As the leaves start to change colour so comes another sign of the onset of autumn – flocks of woodpigeons and sometimes stock doves on the wing. They are on their way to find feeding sites where they can fatten up in preparation for the food shortages of winter. The sight is more common now than in the past. Woodpigeons were once numerous only in deciduous woods, but over the last 150 years or so these adaptable birds have increased in numbers and expanded their range northwards through Britain and Scandinavia.

Urban birds

One reason for this success is the ability of woodpigeons to cope with the increasingly urban landscape of Britain. As native forests have given way first to farms and then to suburbs and new towns, the woodpigeon has found new places to nest in urban centres and parks, in small copses, in hedges and even on the ground. While the growth of intensive farming has reduced nesting places in the country, towns have offered good alternatives.

▲ From a distance, the commonly seen woodpigeon appears to be predominantly grey, with a white neck patch, but closer inspection reveals the more brownish grey back and blushed pink breast.

◄ Unlike the woodpigeon, the smaller, slighter and far less abundant stock dove lacks any white in its plumage.

DID YOU KNOW?
The feathers of pigeons and doves are coated with powder that is used to maintain plumage. If a bird collides with a window, the dust adheres to the glass, leaving a clear print of the body and wings. These marks were once thought to be made by owls as they were usually found in the early morning. However, pigeons are often out and about with the first light.

WOODPIGEON FACT FILE

This large, heavy chested, long-tailed pigeon forages in large flocks during the morning and evening. It takes off with a loud clattering of wings, revealing conspicuous white wing crescents in flight.

● **NAMES**
Common name: woodpigeon
Scientific name: *Columba palumbus*

● **HABITAT**
Anywhere with trees

● **DISTRIBUTION**
Very common; absent from mountains and northern and western isles

● **SIZE**
Length 40–42cm (16–16½in); weight 480–550g (16¾–19½oz)

● **STATUS**
Increasing; no reliable estimate but may be 2,600,000 breeding pairs in Britain and 1,000,000 pairs in Ireland

● **KEY FEATURES**
Upperparts smoky blue with white neck patch (lacking in juveniles), underparts pinkish grey; eyes yellow, bill yellow with red at base and white fleshy bulge (the 'cere') at the top of bill; legs pink; wings with broad white crescents; white-edged primary feathers and black tail band

● **HABITS**
Nodding walking gait; usually focus on one food item

● **VOICE**
Various cooing calls; song '*coo-roo-coo, cor-oo-oo-coo*' with emphasis on second note, repeated with falling phrase at end; individual variation

● **FOOD**
Grain, green leaves, shoots, seeds, berries, acorns, fruit, root crops; occasionally invertebrates

● **BREEDING**
April–September, earlier if enough food available; 2 broods, sometimes 1 or 3

● **NEST**
Flimsy, criss-cross twig structure, usually sited 2–7m (6½–23ft) off ground in tree fork, sometimes in thick ground vegetation, under hedge, or on ledge; re-used, becomes bulkier with time

● **EGGS**
Smooth, white eggs; 1–2 per clutch; male and female incubate for 17 days

● **YOUNG**
Fed crop milk for first week; supply reduced as other foods provided; fledge at 16–34 days, cared for by parents for further week

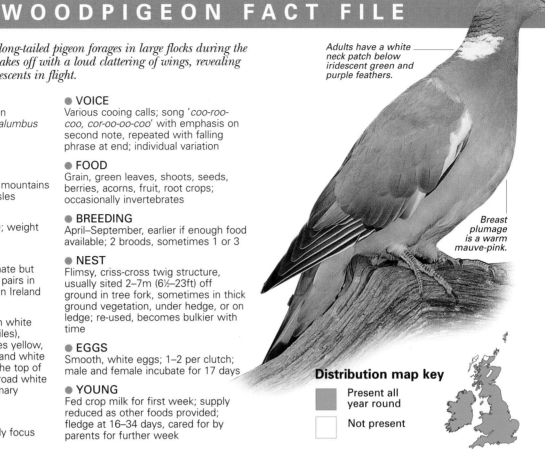

Adults have a white neck patch below iridescent green and purple feathers.

Breast plumage is a warm mauve-pink.

Distribution map key

■ Present all year round

□ Not present

STOCK DOVE FACT FILE

Less numerous than the woodpigeon, the stock dove often feeds in town parks and gardens. Unless in a group, it prefers to stay off the ground and spends much of its time up among the branches of trees.

● **NAMES**
Common name: stock dove
Scientific name: *Columba oenas*

● **HABITAT**
Trees, old buildings and quarries

● **DISTRIBUTION**
Throughout England and Wales and much of Ireland; in Scotland, mainly central lowlands and on east coast

● **SIZE**
Length 32–34cm (12¾–13½in); weight 290–330g (10¼–11½oz)

● **STATUS**
Increasing; estimated 240,000 breeding pairs in Britain, more than 90% in England, and 5000-7000 in Ireland

● **KEY FEATURES**
Plumage mainly blue-grey; wings with two short black bars; flight feathers black-tipped; rump grey; bill yellow or whitish with red at base and small white cere, legs bright pinkish red

● **HABITS**
Less gregarious than woodpigeon, keeps to trees unless in flock

● **VOICE**
Gruff, resonant '*ooo-woo*' uttered 7–10 times or more; often repeated every 1–2 minutes

● **FOOD**
Chiefly seeds, buds, flowers; fresh shoots and leaves gathered in spring by clambering among twigs

● **BREEDING**
Breeding may start late February, if food plentiful; last clutches early October; 1–2 or even 3 broods per year; egg dumping occurs where nest sites in short supply

● **NEST**
Lays eggs in cavities or crevices in trees, cliffs, buildings, or under bush on ground; adds very little nest material; nestboxes adopted readily

● **EGGS**
Usually 2 smooth, white eggs; hatch in 16–18 days; female incubates, male takes over when she feeds

● **YOUNG**
Chicks fed on crop milk for first week or so; fledge in 20–30 days; independent soon afterwards

Distribution map key

■ Present all year round

□ Not present

Iridescent emerald green-blue neck patches show up against the blue-grey plumage of the head and body.

On the upper wings, two small dark bars are even more conspicuous in flight.

The legs are bright pinkish red.

WOODPIGEON AND STOCK DOVE CALENDAR

MARCH • JUNE

In towns, where both species can find a good food supply, first breeding attempts may be under way by March. Birds remain in flocks when feeding and many will still be roosting communally.

JULY • AUGUST

This is the peak breeding season for rural birds, when ripening cereal crops provide plenty of food for hungry youngsters. Their large bills are ideal for taking crop milk from their parents.

SEPTEMBER • OCTOBER

Youngsters continue to fledge until the end of October or even later, and large flocks often gather on suitable fields – especially those where the cereals remain unharvested.

NOVEMBER • FEBRUARY

As days shorten, many stock doves remain in urban areas where they can feed in woods and parks on acorns and beech mast. Others visit fields to eat crops such as cabbages.

The woodpigeon's long breeding season, which lasts from April to October or longer – some birds even nest in winter – is another reason for success. In towns, woodpigeons generally lay earlier than those on farmland. The latter rear their young at harvest time. The adults feed well on vegetable matter and then nourish their young – or 'squabs' – with a nutritious fluid made from the lining of a pouch, or crop, in their throats. This is known as crop milk or pigeon's milk.

Food in winter

During cold weather, when natural food is scarce, agricultural land provides woodpigeons with an excellent opportunity to feed. In particular, winter-growing vegetables are quickly devoured, especially when the tops protrude above snow. This liking for farm produce means that woodpigeons are regarded as serious pests in many areas. Many are shot every year, although whether shooting is an effective method of control is debatable. Farmers aside, woodpigeons have few natural enemies other than the rare goshawk and other occasional predators, ranging from peregrines to foxes.

The stock dove has also spread widely in the last 150 years. Early in the 19th century they were found only in south-eastern England, but they have now found their way to many new areas. In the 1950s and early 1960s, the use of toxic chemical seed dressings caused their numbers to decline, but they are still found in a wide range of habitats, nesting wherever there are old trees with suitable

Vertical launch

The woodpigeon can take off almost vertically from the ground. With a leap upwards and a sweep downwards it springs into the air in a manner that is more efficient than graceful.

First sinking into a squat, the woodpigeon uses its powerful thigh muscles to thrust itself upwards.

As it stretches up, its wings are raised very high, and then brought down rapidly to give instant lift.

With wings beating in great, deep strokes, take-off is quick and agile.

The stock dove is the only pigeon to nest regularly in holes in old trees, often in crevices once used by woodpeckers. Stock doves will also nest in holes in buildings or on cliffs, under bushes or even in burrows.

holes, in holes in cliffs or quarries or old buildings with likely crevices, although numbers have probably not yet reached pre-1950 levels. The stock dove's recovery is helped by crops of winter barley, which provide it with food.

Over the short term, the major determinant of woodpigeon and stock dove populations is the weather. Cold winters reduce the birds' chances of survival. When snow covers feeding grounds, birds gather in dense groups on the few clear patches of earth, and this can encourage outbreaks of a parasitic disease. A tiny worm called *Trichomonas gallinae* infects the birds' throats and eventually causes them to starve because they are unable to swallow any food. The condition is not usually as serious as this, but diseased birds pass on the infection as the food they are unable to swallow is spat out and picked up by others in the flock.

Aerial display

The woodpigeon is a powerful flier with a repertoire of manoeuvres that includes a variety of accomplished escape tactics. It is able to employ rapid turns and swerves and tumbling falls to avoid predators such as the goshawk. In summer, the woodpigeon marks its territory and attempts to attract females by uttering a special advertising call and indulging in an impressively acrobatic display flight.

In this the bird flies forward and upward, rising slowly, and then suddenly ascends steeply and at the apex of the ascent makes a loud, clapping sound with its wings. The bird then glides down again on stiffly held wings with its tail fanned. This impressive performance may take place up to five times before the male bird lands, at which time it will raise and lower its tail several times.

The stock dove also performs a display flight in spring or summer, but one that is more like that of the rock dove. The male

Attention seeking

The male woodpigeon's display flight begins with a steep climb up to about 10m (33ft) – followed by a spectacular near-vertical ascent.

Using powerful wing strokes, the male rises high in the air in order to make itself as conspicuous as possible, before announcing its presence with a loud wing clap. In display flights, males aim to be noticed by rival males as well as females.

may fly in a large circle, with its wings held in a shallow 'V', giving rather slow, deep wing beats to produce a quieter wing clap. A grumbling display call is used on the ground, the male fluffing out his neck feathers while bowing to the female.

Feasting flocks

When the flocks gather in autumn, most of the birds will have come just a few kilometres, or miles. About half the recoveries of ringed woodpigeons in Britain are found within 10km (6 miles) of their original capture. Stock doves show similar sedentary tendencies, but there are three records of British-ringed stock doves turning up in France and Spain. On the Continent, by contrast, huge movements of stock doves occur as they fly from cold and snowy areas to the south-west, often over the Pyrenees.

Many people believe that large numbers of migrant woodpigeons visit Britain during the autumn and early winter. In fact, most of these birds, which are smaller and duller than the usual native species, are not foreign visitors, but youngsters that have hatched in Britain late in the year. Very few birds travel across the North Sea, nor do many venture across the Channel.

WILDLIFE WATCH

Where can I see woodpigeons and stock doves?

● Woodpigeons are large, conspicuous and easy to see. Not only are they becoming increasingly common, but they are moving in to suburban and even urban areas. The birds frequent parks and gardens and can even be seen at birdfeeders, despite modern seed mixes generally being formulated for smaller species. Traditional mixes using large seeds and cereals will attract more woodpigeons.

● Agricultural land can attract up to 2000 woodpigeons and stock doves – sometimes as many as 10,000 – in autumn and winter.

● Look for woodpigeons around ivy in the early spring, from late February onwards, when they flock to gorge themselves on the new spring berries.

● It is often possible to spot hundreds of woodpigeon nests in a well-grown conifer plantation. Their flimsy nests are often the most common structures in the trees and are not concealed at all.

● Stock doves can easily be overlooked. They often join woodpigeons in mixed flocks, although they also gather in single species flocks of up to 200 birds or occasionally more. Grey feral pigeons are quite similar in size and appearance, but their white rumps, the lack of a thick black border around the rear of the wings and longer black bars on the upper wings are clear markers.

In severe weather, a woodpigeon will turn its attention to cabbages or other brassicas such as these Brussels sprouts. The damage caused at such times has earned woodpigeons the status of pest on farms.

The nuthatch

This lively bird works hard to collect a winter store of nuts and seeds, which it guards jealously from rivals. Hopping confidently, the nuthatch's strong feet often carry it headfirst down the trunk.

At first glance, the nuthatch looks rather like a small woodpecker, in both its shape and the way it moves among the trees. It has short, powerful legs with strong feet and curved claws that are perfect for climbing. This beautiful little bird is at home patrolling the trunks of trees, and also regularly feeds while dangling from the most slender branches of the upper canopy. It sometimes ventures to the ground, especially in spring and autumn. In fact, the diminutive nuthatch is more adroit than any woodpecker, because it not only climbs vertically, but it can also reverse direction and head for the ground. This behaviour, unknown in any other British bird species, is especially beneficial when the nuthatch is investigating crevices closely in its search for food.

Familiar haunts

Despite its woodpecker-like behaviour, the nuthatch is more closely allied to the tit family. It is found in deciduous woods in central and southern England and Wales. It also breeds in established parkland with old trees and often visits mature trees in nearby gardens. The species declined in northern Britain in the 19th century, but in recent years its range has expanded northwards once more. Cumbria has been colonised in the last 70 or so years and a few pairs are now starting to breed in Scotland. Colonisation of new areas is slow, however, because the nuthatch is mainly a sedentary species. In Britain, nuthatches seldom travel great distances from the trees where they hatched. Pairs remain in their territories for the whole year and their young do not disperse far to set up their own ranges.

Nuthatches are often extremely noisy. Their loud '*tuit, tuit, tuit*' call is frequently the first clue that the birds are present. It may be heard at any time of year and is usually delivered by a bird defending its territory. The nuthatch also utters a loud trill, which is most often heard in spring. The sound has been likened to a referee's whistle that is partly blocked, giving more of a rattle than a whistle.

In winter, unpaired birds also maintain individual territories, but these are much smaller than those of breeding birds. A resident pair may tolerate a third bird, perhaps a juvenile, inside their normal territorial boundaries. Nuthatches sometimes join a roving feeding flock with tits and other small birds while the flock is within their territory. However, they are unlikely to go beyond their own territorial boundaries.

As spring approaches, nest building begins. The nuthatch does not use its beak in the manner of a woodpecker for chiselling out a hole in which to nest. Instead, like most tits, it inhabits a natural recess in a tree or takes over an old woodpecker hole. It may even use an available nestbox.

◄ Most of the nuthatch's food consists of beetles and other small insects found on the trunk and in branches of trees. This agile bird frequently feeds upside down, a rearward pointing claw helping to keep it securely attached to the tree bark.

NUTHATCH FACT FILE

A perky little songbird, the nuthatch has a sleek, compact but sturdy body with a large head, short tail and powerful spear-like bill. Not at all shy, its bluish back and contrasting chestnut flanks may be seen in parks and gardens as it darts among the trees on broad wings.

● NAMES
Common names: nuthatch, Eurasian nuthatch, wood nuthatch
Scientific name: *Sitta europaea*

● HABITAT
Deciduous woods, copses on farms and in parks, mature parkland and gardens with large trees

● DISTRIBUTION
Most common in central and southern England and Wales; has started colonising Scotland

● SIZE
Length 14cm (5½in); weight 22–25g (¾–1oz)

● STATUS
Estimated 130,000 territories

● KEY FEATURES
Upperparts bluish grey; underparts rusty buff; white spots on undertail; flanks and undertail are darker red-chestnut in males; head large, rather flat and long, with strong black, pointed bill; thick black eyestripe; tail and legs short

● HABITS
Clings to tree trunks and branches; climbs in short, jerky hops

● VOICE
Call is a loud *'tuit, tuit, tuit'*; song, heard mainly in spring, is a loud, rattling *'pee, pee, pee'* trill

● FOOD
Mainly small beetles and other insects, also spiders, during summer; nuts and seeds at other times, especially hazelnuts in autumn

● BREEDING
Eggs laid mainly late April–late May; 1, rarely 2, broods

● NEST
Holes in trees and walls or nestboxes; mud-plastered entrance

● EGGS
Usually 6–8 eggs, white with dark, reddish brown marks; incubated by female for 14–15 days

● YOUNG
Fledge at 23–25 days

▲ **From late April to mid-June, the nuthatch rears its young. A pair often chooses a hole in a tree as a nest site. The female lines the bottom of the cavity with flakes of bark and dried leaves.**

▶ **The nuthatch instinctively plasters mud around the entrance to its nest hole, even if it has chosen a nestbox. The mud is so strong that ornithologists have to use a hammer and chisel to open the boxes for cleaning at the end of summer.**

Distribution map key

███ Present all year round

☐ Not present

Blackish flight feathers of wing contrast with paler bluish grey upperparts.

Beneath a black eyestripe, the face and upper throat are white.

Rusty buff underparts darken to a deep chestnut colour on the flanks and undertail of the male.

Strong legs and feet are set well back on the body, and curved claws are big and sharp.

STORING NUTS

In summer, the nuthatch eats insects, such as beetles, and spiders, but in autumn and winter it lives on nuts and seeds. This ingenious bird does not use its strong, spike-like bill to chisel into tree trunks to find food, unless the wood is rotten, but hacks open the hard outer cases of nuts and seeds to get at the protein-rich kernels. A nuthatch takes the food item and wedges it in a small crevice in a tree.

Once the nut or seed is secure, the bird delivers several sharp blows to its surface until the outer shell cracks and the edible interior is revealed.

The nuthatch's method of dealing with food has given the species its common English name. It has also resulted in some interesting country names, including the 'woodcracker'. In Surrey it was known as the 'woodhacker', and in Shropshire as the 'nutcracker'.

Some of the food items opened are surprisingly tough, including hazelnuts, acorns, yew seeds and pine cones. There are even reports of nuthatches picking out undigested seeds from the droppings of other birds and animals and cracking them open.

Nuthatches are great hoarders of food. In autumn, they take advantage of the seasonal abundance of nuts and seeds to cache supplies in anticipation of harsh weather to come. This is an important survival strategy for a bird that rarely travels far when foraging. It is also a good reason for the birds to continue to maintain their territories throughout the winter, as they can then prevent other birds from raiding their secret stores.

◀ **Nuts such as hazel, beech and acorns are jammed into the bark of a tree, then split open, either at the time or later, when food is harder to find.**

▶ **The presence of a nuthatch is often revealed by the loud tapping noises made as the bird hammers vigorously at a nut it has wedged into a crevice in a tree.**

Tree life

The nuthatch spends most of its life off the ground. Its territory is generally centred around a network of mature deciduous trees, which provide all its needs. The nuthatch forages for food by scuttling around the tree and sometimes also finds a home by locating a hole and modifying the entrance to its own specification.

Unlike woodpeckers or treecreepers, the nuthatch does not use its tail for support, but instead relies upon its robust feet and big sharp claws. It grips the bark with one foot and braces itself with the other.

The nuthatch collects tiny beads of mud to cement the opening of its nest hole, making several journeys to and from nearby muddy puddles.

The natural holes that are favoured by nuthatches are also popular with other, larger woodland birds, especially starlings. These will readily oust a pair of nesting nuthatches if they have the opportunity. To overcome this problem, the nuthatch gathers large amounts of mud, which it plasters around the entrance to the nest hole until eventually the opening is reduced far to a size that will allow the rightful occupant to enter, but is too small for starlings or other larger birds to use for access.

Once the nest hole has been selected, the female busies herself filling the cavity with large amounts of dead leaves, wood chippings and pieces of bark. Jigsaw-shaped flakes of bark from the Scots pine are particularly popular, and birds may travel 800m (half a mile) or so to find a good source. The female plasters the inside and outside of the cavity with pellets of wet mud or clay, which she then hammers into shape with her bill. This nest building usually takes two to three weeks.

When a nuthatch uses a nestbox, it encounters an interesting predicament. Most nestboxes have a hole that is exactly the right size for a great tit and so also the correct size for a nuthatch. Therefore

A nuthatch is not limited to hunting for food among tree branches. This adaptable bird has been observed hovering like a hummingbird to pick tiny aphids from the tips of ash leaves to feed to its young.

there is no need to make it smaller. However, the nuthatch's instinct to use mud is very strong, and this urge often results in the bird plastering around the hole, sealing up any cracks and even cementing the box to the tree.

The female incubates the eggs alone and when she takes a break, she will often cover her clutch with nest material. Once the young hatch, they are fed by both of their parents.

Rosy future

Many parks have wooded areas and most of Britain's remaining woodland is now safeguarded, so the future looks promising for the nuthatch. Its movement northwards seems set to continue and, in time, it is likely that this tree-loving bird will both increase in numbers and expand its range still farther.

▶ **A considerable supply of insects, provided by both parents, is eaten by the hungry nuthatch young. The chicks' bills are full of saliva, which is thought to aid swallowing the insects' hard exoskeletons.**

NUTHATCH CALENDAR

MARCH ● APRIL

As the weather becomes milder, the nuthatch's loud and rattling song is often heard. The birds select a suitable nesting hole and defend it from all rivals. The first clutches are laid in April.

MAY ● JUNE

The eggs are incubated by the female alone, and after 14 to 15 days the chicks hatch. The youngsters grow quickly on a protein-rich diet of insects provided by both parents.

JULY ● OCTOBER

The young fledge but continue to be fed by their parents. Eventually, they disperse in search of territories of their own. The adults go through a complete moult and begin to hide stores of nuts and seeds.

NOVEMBER ● FEBRUARY

Food is more difficult to find, so the birds exploit their hidden stores. They join mixed species feeding flocks and travel with them, but do not venture outside their own ranges.

◀ **Autumn is the season when a nuthatch is most likely to be seen on the ground. When there is a glut of food, it will store more than it can eat and is often seen carrying nuts and seeds away to its hiding place.**

WILDLIFE WATCH

Where can I see nuthatches?

● In a few public parks, such as Richmond Park and Kew Gardens in Surrey, nuthatches have become accustomed to people. Some of the birds will come close to humans – even to the hand – for food.

● Nuthatches may visit gardens that are close to mature parkland and contain old trees. They can be attracted by putting out birdfeeders full of peanuts or sunflower seeds.

● Most large woodlands in southern Britain harbour nuthatches, but patience and luck are needed to locate them. They are very noisy for small birds, so listen for them in spring, before there are too many leaves on the trees to obscure their presence.

● Woodland reserves that are looked after by The Royal Society for the Protection of Birds (RSPB), such as Chapel Wood in Devon, Blean Woods in Kent, The Lodge in Bedfordshire, Nagshead in Gloucestershire, and Coombes Valley in Staffordshire, all have good populations of nuthatches.

Recognising slugs

These relentless consumers of fungi and decaying vegetable matter are often on the move after a shower of rain. They use a flattened, muscular foot coated with thick mucus to progress through grass, along the ground and even up walls.

Autumn is the best time to see slugs because rainy weather often brings them out during the day. In drier weather, slugs emerge above ground only at night, when the air is relatively cool and damp.

This behaviour stems from the fact that their soft, unprotected bodies can easily dry out. To avoid dessication, slugs seek out dank places. In periods of drought, they squeeze into crevices and burrow deeper underground

to where the soil remains moist. During the summer months, slugs can be found up to a metre (yard) below the surface.

Britain and Ireland are home to numerous species, ranging in size from the diminutive 3cm (1¼in) long chestnut slug to the ash-grey slug that has been known to reach a length of 30cm (12in).

Like snails, slugs are gastropods – which means 'belly feet', and refers to the way the animals move around on their bellies. Snails have a tough shell into which they can retract their bodies for protection and to reduce water loss. Slugs do not have such a covering and rely on a

slimy coating of mucus to shield them from dessication, and to help them move.

Living quarters

Slugs are found in many different places, including parks, gardens, woodland, farmland, heaths, hedgerows and mountains – one species even lives in trees, and is called the tree slug. Parks with plenty of trees and woodlands are the most productive places for a slug-hunt. Some species favour ancient, undisturbed areas, while others can be found in open clearings, rides and along the sides of fields.

Most of the slugs encountered in urban parks and gardens also occur along the edges of open spaces. The clearing of woodland to create cultivated land – both farms and gardens – has

undoubtedly helped the spread of slug species. Under natural conditions, slugs tend to consume decaying vegetable matter and fungi. The relatively tough and unpalatable leaves of most healthy wild plants are avoided by all slugs. However, in parks and gardens and on farms, cultivars with soft, nutritious leaves represent ideal food for slugs. As well as leaves they eat flowers, fruit, bulbs and tubers.

Even so, only a small number of slug species are regarded as pests – the rest feed harmlessly on fungi, decaying plant matter or even small invertebrates.

WILDLIFE WATCH

Where can I see slugs?

● In town and country, parks and parkland are often full of slugs, especially after rain. They also come out after dark. Use a torch to search carefully in woods and gardens.

● Slugs climb quite high up trees to graze on algae, lichens and fungi growing on the bark.

● Look for slugs on wood or rocks bearing algae or fungi. Look for them, too, on and around rotting vegetation, which they also like to eat.

● Search in and around mature compost heaps for the curious shelled slug, which, as its name suggests, has a tiny shell, resembling a fingernail, on its back.

Black slugs are not always black – they occur in several colour forms, including orange, as shown here. These large slugs are common visitors to gardens.

EASY GUIDE TO SPOTTING SLUGS

WHAT ARE SLUGS?

● Gastropods belonging to the subclass Pulmonata, slugs have a 'lung' beneath the mantle, which is a conspicuous raised area of skin behind the head. This opens via a breathing pore, allowing the passage of air in and out of the body.

● Slugs lack a fully formed external shell but most have an internal shell – usually located under the mantle – the size and shape of which varies. Shells of slugs belonging to the family Arionidae have degenerated to just a few remnants and in some cases to merely a few chalky granules. Slugs belonging to the family Testacellidae do have an external shell, but this is very small and underdeveloped.

● Thick mucus makes slugs' bodies extremely slimy and helps them to move easily across the ground. It also acts as a 'glue' so that they can climb vertical surfaces.

● Eyes are positioned at the end of two tentacles. Two shorter tentacles help slugs to detect food by smell and taste.

● Each slug has both male and female sex organs. However, mating normally occurs between two individuals, allowing cross-fertilisation.

● Surprisingly long-lived, some slugs survive for several years.

HOW CAN I IDENTIFY SLUGS?

● Slugs found in the British Isles belong to seven genera, each of which has distinctive characteristics that allow identification in the field. One of them, *Boettgerilla*, is found in Ireland and the Channel Isles only. Having determined the genus to which a slug belongs, take a closer look at its body. Important features to notice include the mantle, the texture of the body and the tentacles.

● Members of the genus *Arion* have a mantle that appears smooth or finely pitted. The body has ridges along its length but lacks a dorsal keel, which is a distinct line extending along the centre of the body from the tail.

● Slugs of the genus *Limax* have a 'fingerprint' pattern on the mantle, centred on the mid-line of the body. There is a short keel at the tail end and the tail itself tapers.

● Members of the genus *Testacella* have a small external shell near the tip of the tail.

● *Deroceras* slugs have a 'fingerprint' pattern on the mantle but, unlike the *Limax*, it is centred around the breathing pore. There is a short keel at the tail end and the tail is abruptly truncated, turning down sharply at the tip.

● *Geomalacus* slugs have distinctive spots and these slugs curl into a ball if disturbed. Just one species is found in the British Isles and this is limited to Ireland.

● The genus *Milax* comprises slugs with a keel that extends from the tail to the mantle. The mantle surface is roughly textured and marked with a horseshoe-shaped groove.

Distribution map key

 Present all year round

 Not present

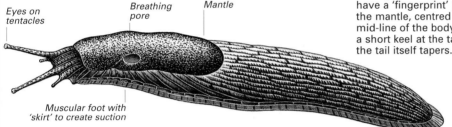

Eyes on tentacles
Breathing pore
Mantle
Muscular foot with 'skirt' to create suction

LARGE BLACK SLUG *Arion ater*

Also known as the large red slug, this species occurs in black, orange-red and yellowish grey forms. Adults are uniformly coloured, but young slugs may be striped and are always pale. The fringe of the foot is often reddish.

The large black slug's body is marked with prominent ridges. If it is disturbed, it normally hunches up and withdraws its tentacles.

● SIZE
Up to 15cm (6in) long

● MUCUS
Colourless

● FOOD
Mainly dead and decaying vegetable matter but will eat garden plants

● SEASON
Active all year round, especially in wet weather

● HABITAT
Wooded and grassy places, including mountains and gardens

● DISTRIBUTION
Throughout British Isles

COMMON GARDEN SLUG *Arion hortensis* complex

A variably patterned slug, its body is grey, brownish or black and may bear lines of orange-brown spots. The sole of the foot is yellow or orange-brown. *Arion hortensis* probably comprises a group of three species.

This slug's body surface is furrowed. Tentacles may be blackish or reddish in colour.

● SIZE
Up to 3cm (1¼in), rarely 4cm (1½in) long

● MUCUS
Orange-yellow

● FOOD
Mainly decaying vegetable matter, but also seedlings

● SEASON
Mainly autumn to spring

● HABITAT
Gardens, open woodland and agricultural land – widely regarded as a pest

● DISTRIBUTION
Throughout British Isles, but scarce or absent from some high-altitude areas

DUSKY SLUG *Arion subfuscus*

This distinctive slug has an orange-brown to dark brown body with conspicuous dark stripes along its length. The sole is yellowish. The body does not contract fully when the slug is disturbed.

Dusky slugs are best looked for in autumn. At this time, they are feeding on fresh crops of seasonal fungi.

● **SIZE**
Up to 7cm (2¾in) long

● **MUCUS**
Bright yellow or orange; will stain fingers if touched

● **FOOD**
Decaying vegetable matter and fungi

● **SEASON**
All year round; most easily found in autumn

● **HABITAT**
Woodland, hedgerows, fields, dunes and gardens

● **DISTRIBUTION**
Throughout the British Isles; rare in East Anglia

SILVER SLUG *Arion silvaticus*

Delicate and compact, the silver slug has a pale greyish body, with a broad dark stripe along each flank. The mantle is speckled buffish yellow, the tentacles are dark and the sole is a whitish colour.

Like many woodland slugs, the silver slug can often be found wandering over tree bark. It grazes on algae and small fungi from the bark's surface.

● **SIZE**
Up to 4cm (1½in) long

● **MUCUS**
Colourless

● **FOOD**
Mainly dead and decaying vegetable matter and fungi

● **SEASON**
Most active in autumn and winter

● **HABITAT**
Woods, heaths, grassland and farmland; sometimes found in gardens

● **DISTRIBUTION**
Throughout the British Isles

ASH-GREY SLUG *Limax cinereoniger*

The ash-grey is the largest slug to be found in the British Isles. It has been known to reach 30cm (12in) in length. Its body is usually dark ashy grey with a paler keel. The sole of the foot is dark with a white central line.

Often orange in colour, the keel of the ash-grey slug runs from the mantle to the tail, two-thirds of its body length.

● **SIZE**
20cm (8in) or more long

● **MUCUS**
Colourless

● **FOOD**
Dead and decaying leaf material and its associated fungi

● **SEASON**
All year round

● **HABITAT**
Undisturbed places, especially in ancient woodland

● **DISTRIBUTION**
Local in western parts and southern England

LEOPARD SLUG OR GREAT GREY SLUG *Limax maximus*

Large and strikingly marked, the leopard slug has a pinkish grey body, with two or three horizontal dark bands, often broken up into spots. It has a short keel and the sole of the foot is whitish.

The leopard slug's markings provide excellent camouflage among vegetation. It frequently occurs in gardens.

● **SIZE**
Up to 20cm (8in) long

● **MUCUS**
Colourless and sticky

● **FOOD**
Eats only decaying vegetable matter

● **SEASON**
All year round

● **HABITAT**
Hedgerows, garden undergrowth and damp woodland

● **DISTRIBUTION**
Throughout British Isles

TREE SLUG *Limax marginatus*

This medium-sized slug has a pale greyish buff body that looks rather gelatinous. It can appear almost translucent in wet weather. It usually has dark longitudinal body bands, two of which extend on to the mantle in a lyre shape. There is a rare spotted form.

As its name suggests, this slug may often be found climbing trees to feed.

● **SIZE**
Up to 8cm (3in) long

● **MUCUS**
Colourless, thin and watery; usually produced in copious amounts

● **FOOD**
Lichens, algae and fungi

● **SEASON**
Autumn and winter

● **HABITAT**
Mainly woodland with mature trees

● **DISTRIBUTION**
Absent from or scarce in eastern England, but widespread elsewhere

LEMON SLUG *Limax tenellus*

The lemon slug is an attractive species with a yellow body that appears gelatinous and translucent. There is usually a faint darker band along each side. The tentacles are dark, often purple, and the sole is whitish.

This slug's appearance in autumn coincides with a bonanza of mushrooms and toadstools, on which it feeds almost exclusively.

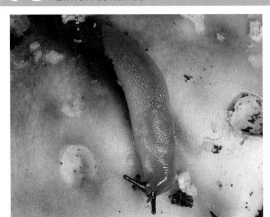

● **SIZE**
Up to 4cm (1½in) long

● **MUCUS**
Yellow or orange in copious amounts

● **FOOD**
Feeds mainly on woodland fungi

● **SEASON**
Autumn and early winter

● **HABITAT**
Mature and undisturbed woodland; often found under beech trees but also under conifers

● **DISTRIBUTION**
Scattered patches from south-eastern England to central Scotland

YELLOW SLUG *Limax flavus*

Often associated with human habitation and gardens, the yellow slug may even venture indoors. Its large and distinctive body is usually yellow mottled with grey and it has prominent pale blue tentacles.

Lettuce leaves are a favourite food of the yellow slug. It tends to choose leaves that have already been slightly damaged.

● **SIZE**
Up to 10cm (4in) long

● **MUCUS**
Body slime is yellow; foot slime is colourless

● **FOOD**
Seedlings, shoots and decaying vegetable matter

● **SEASON**
All year round

● **HABITAT**
Mainly gardens; often found in outhouses and cellars

● **DISTRIBUTION**
Widespread, but in Scotland only in the south

SHELLED SLUG *Testacella scutulum*

One of three British species of shelled slugs, this one has a small translucent shell located on top of its body, towards the rear end. The upper body is yellowish, with darker speckles, while the sole and the edge of the foot are orange.

The lumpy-looking shelled slug feeds on earthworms and small invertebrates found in the soil.

● **SIZE**
Up to 10cm (4in) long

● **MUCUS**
Colourless

● **FOOD**
Carnivorous; prey comprises mostly earthworms

● **SEASON**
All year round

● **HABITAT**
Parks and gardens; mainly in soil or mature compost heaps

● **DISTRIBUTION**
Local in south and south-eastern England and south-eastern Ireland

CHESTNUT SLUG *Deroceras panormitanum* (or *Deroceras caruanae*)

An unusually active species, the chestnut slug is aggressive to others of its kind and occasionally even cannibalistic. Its body is greyish brown with a chestnut mantle. However, it can appear rather translucent.

The chestnut slug is a pest in parks, gardens and plant nurseries. It was introduced to Britain from Mediterranean countries.

● **SIZE**
Up to 3.5cm (1⅜in) long

● **MUCUS**
Colourless

● **FOOD**
Decaying vegetable matter, also invertebrates, including slugs

● **SEASON**
All year round

● **HABITAT**
Gardens and other cultivated areas

● **DISTRIBUTION**
Found in much of the British Isles and expanding its range

GREY FIELD (OR NETTED) SLUG *Deroceras reticulatum*

Probably the most common slug in lowland Britain and Ireland, the netted slug is a major pest of cultivated plants. Its body is pale brown, but usually marbled and netted with dark veins and blotches. The sole is pale and the keel is short.

This prolific species can devastate crops of cultivated vegetables such as lettuces. Most damage occurs in autumn.

● **SIZE**
Up to 5cm (2in) long

● **MUCUS**
Usually colourless, turns milky when agitated or disturbed

● **FOOD**
All types of vegetable matter, both living and decaying

● **SEASON**
All year round

● **HABITAT**
Gardens and farmland

● **DISTRIBUTION**
Common throughout the British Isles

KERRY SLUG *Geomalacus maculosus*

Impressive and well marked, the Kerry slug is usually dark greenish grey with white or yellow spots. When disturbed, it curls up into a ball. Outside Ireland this species occurs only on the western coasts of Spain and Portugal.

The Kerry slug is the only British species that has such distinctive spots. Juveniles are less well marked.

● **SIZE**
Up to 9cm (3½in) long

● **MUCUS**
Colourless or milky

● **FOOD**
Lichens, mosses and algae

● **SEASON**
All year round, but almost impossible to find in dry summer weather

● **HABITAT**
Lichen and moss-covered boulders and trees

● **DISTRIBUTION**
Found in south-western Ireland only

BUDAPEST SLUG *Milax budapestensis*

An abundant and serious pest of crops, the Budapest slug has spread from its native range in eastern Europe via human activities. Its variably coloured body contrasts with an orange keel. The sole of the foot is yellowish white, usually with a dark central line.

The Budapest slug may nibble lettuce leaves but it eats mainly root crops.

● **SIZE**
Up to 6cm (2½in) long

● **MUCUS**
Colourless

● **FOOD**
Mainly root crops; also young shoots and seedlings and decaying vegetable matter

● **SEASON**
All year round

● **HABITAT**
Gardens, farmland and other cultivated ground

● **DISTRIBUTION**
Widespread but absent from northern Scotland

Weevils

Recognisable by their long snouts and distinctive jointed antennae, weevils are the most diverse and numerous of all beetles. Some are a glossy black, others spotted or striped, while yet others shimmer with a green glow.

If evolutionary success is measured by number of species, then weevils are the most successful animals on the planet. There are more species of weevils in the world than all the mammal, bird, reptile and amphibian species added together. More than 50,000 species have been scientifically described, and this is only a fraction of the total. Europe has more than 1500 known species, of which more than 580 are found in the British Isles.

Weevils are basically beetles with snouts, although the length of snout varies enormously. It can be so short that it hardly merits the name, or so long that it projects way out in front of the insect's face in a graceful, arching, downward curve, like that of the acorn weevil. At the tip of the snout – more correctly called the rostrum – are tiny but efficient mouthparts. These are capable of biting substantial holes into quite hard materials such as wood. The antennae are usually attached to the snout and 'elbowed' in a very characteristic way. Many species are flightless, and their wing cases are fused together into one piece.

Iridescent gleam

Most British weevils are very small – just 3–4mm (⅛in) long – and some are quite attractive, such as the iridescent green weevils of the genus *Phyllobius*. They include the nettle weevil, *Phyllobius pomaceus*, which is often abundant on those plants, and other green or coppery species that are frequently found on parkland trees and shrubs. Many species of weevils are common in autumn.

All weevils have elongated snouts, but the slender, curved snout of the acorn weevil is as long as the rest of its body. The way that the 'elbowed' antennae sprout from each side of the snout is typical of weevils.

Nearly all weevils eat just vegetable matter. Adults and larvae feed on the leaves, stems, fruit and seeds of a huge variety of plants. One of the most common seed-eaters in Britain is the gorse weevil, found on gorse from Cornwall to northern Scotland. The tiny, silvery grey, black and brown adults can often be found on gorse plants in parkland with acid soils. The female lays her eggs among the seeds of the gorse, but first she must use her long rostrum to bore a hole in a young gorse pod. This can take her several hours, but eventually she turns around, backs into the hole and deposits about six eggs. Throughout the summer the larvae feed on the seeds within the pod. They pupate and emerge in late summer as adults. Although quite capable of boring their way out, they wait until the gorse pods burst naturally – with an audible crack – shooting seeds and any occupying weevils in all directions. The weevils feed through autumn before hibernating for the winter.

Nut nurseries

The female nut weevil uses her sharp mouthparts to gnaw a deep hole in a developing hazelnut, the kernel of which will provide a nutritious meal for her larvae. Her rostrum is extremely long, enabling her to penetrate deep into the nut. The very similar acorn weevil uses the same technique on acorns, but the

The bright colours of *Phyllobius* weevils, such as this one, are caused by reflections from iridescent scales that cover the black wing cases. These scales gradually wear, so older individuals can look quite bald and dark.

MATING GAMES

Weevils are often discovered in mounted pairs, although they seldom appear to be actually mating. The average female weevil seems to be reluctant to mate, forcing a male to spend many hours perched rather precariously on her back, in anticipation that she will eventually permit him to couple up. His persistence pays off, however, since he can be reasonably confident that any eggs she lays will be fertilised by him alone. Male insects that have a more perfunctory courtship have no such guarantee.

▶ Males are far more eager to mate than females. It is not unusual to see two males trying to mate with a single female, as in these least green weevils.

◀ Female weevils are so obstinate that males may transfer their attentions to other insects. This coppery tree weevil is apparently trying to mate with the wrong end of a seven-spot ladybird.

▶ A male may spend more than an hour trying to persuade a female to mate, while she tries repeatedly to dislodge him with her back legs. These are clay-coloured weevils, which can be common in parks.

▲ At up to 13mm (⅝in) long, the pine weevil is a giant among British weevils. The adults feed on young pine shoots, often fatally wounding young trees. The weevil larvae live in dead tree stumps.

grey oak weevil opts to lay its eggs in the galls caused on oaks by small wasps. The bean gall weevil does the same on willows, laying its eggs in the early stages of galls induced by sawflies. In some areas, almost half of the bean galls will contain such an invader rather than the rightful occupant, which will be killed in the process.

Lesser weevils

Weevil larvae usually betray little sign of their presence, as they often feed within roots, stems or fruit. The slug-like larvae of the figwort weevil are an exception, feeding in groups in the open on figwort leaves, which they reduce to skeletons.

Some female weevils build cradles for their young by rolling up suitable leaves. The hazel leaf-rolling weevil spends several hours engaged in the laborious and complex task of converting a hazel leaf into a tight roll. She does this by a series of nips and tucks, weakening the leaf at various strategic points by biting holes in it, before folding it over with her legs and rostrum. These rolls can be very conspicuous, especially when the leaves go brown. Each roll usually contains one egg. The larvae develop very rapidly in their carefully made home, enabling this small but attractive red weevil to produce two generations each year.

▶ Weevil larvae have powerful chewing mouthparts, which enable species such as this nut weevil to feed on nutrient-rich nut kernels. They pupate inside the nuts, and bore their way out as newly formed adults.

▼ The striking hazel leaf-rolling weevil constructs a secure nursery for its young by rolling up the end of a leaf. The female lays a single egg in the resulting tube through a hole carefully snipped in the leaf.

WILDLIFE WATCH

Where can I find weevils?

● Weevils are found wherever there are plants. Several species are common in parks. They include the vine weevil, the larvae of which are notorious for destroying the roots of pot plants. Many are active in autumn, including the figwort weevil and the conspicuously striped pea weevil, which feeds on leguminous plants such as peas and vetches.

● Most British weevils are very small, and have to be found by searching the vegetation. Entomologists carrying out surveys often find weevils and other tiny insects by sweeping with a heavy net, or gently beating them off leaves on to a tray or sheet for a closer look.

The crane-fly

After weeks spent feeding underground as a blind, legless larva, this unmistakable insect lives for just a few days as a winged adult. As the sun sets, swarms of males gather with the sole purpose of attracting a mate.

Clumsy, leggy and looking disturbingly like airborne spiders, crane-flies are extremely common. A stroll through the park in early autumn is likely to flush large numbers of them from the grass, and send them buzzing into the air, where they fly about in an aimless way before settling again. Crane-flies are attracted to lighted windows at night, and frequently get into houses to alarm the occupants with their thin, dangling legs and blundering flight.

About 300 species of crane-flies live in the British Isles, including the largest of all British flies, the giant crane-fly *Tipula maxima*, which has a wingspan of about 65mm (2⅜in). However, most of the

species found in Britain are about the size of a mosquito, from which they are easily distinguished by their shiny, hairless wings and lack of a slender proboscis, or elongated mouthpart.

The three most familiar garden species are considerably larger than this. They are the common crane-fly *Tipula oleracea*, the marsh crane-fly *Tipula paludosa* and the spotted crane-fly *Nephrotoma appendiculata*. The latter is on the wing from May to September and is easily recognised by its striking black and yellow body. The two *Tipula* species are both dull greyish brown and about 25mm (1in) long, and they are not at all easy to distinguish from each other. The marsh crane-fly is most common in the autumn, but both species can be seen on the wing from April through to October.

Legs and wings

Large crane-flies are sometimes known as 'daddy-long-legs', although their weak, spindly legs are of little use for walking and are used simply to cling on to vegetation and other perches. They break

▲ A close view of a giant crane-fly shows the long, club-like projections, or halteres, behind its wings. These sense when the fly lurches in flight, and help it to maintain a straight course.

▼ The common crane-fly has a more silvery grey coloration than the very similar marsh crane-fly. The pointed tail of this individual shows that it is a female.

◄ One of the most familiar park and garden species, the marsh crane-fly's large compound eyes and sensitive antennae help it find a mate and breed.

◄ One of the most familiar park and garden species, the marsh crane-fly's large compound eyes and sensitive antennae help it find a mate and breed.

▼ The crane-fly uses its legs as props to support it when it settles, but it cannot actually walk. To move over a surface, it hovers with legs dangling, giving the impression that it is dancing on tip-toe.

off easily if the insects are handled or caught in spiders' webs, and do not regrow. However, a crane-fly can survive if it retains at least three legs, provided they are not all on the same side of its body.

Like all true flies, crane-flies have just one pair of functional wings. The hind pair is modified into two club-like balancers, called halteres, which act as flight stabilisers. All true flies have these, and they give groups such as hoverflies their remarkable flying skill. Those of crane-flies are particularly long and obvious, but ironically crane-flies fly rather poorly. The females of a few species have only vestigial wings, so they cannot fly at all. When resting, the largest species hold their wings outspread, but most small crane-flies rest with their wings folded flat over their bodies.

The three common species fly mainly at night, and mating pairs can often be seen resting on house walls in the morning. Males and females are easily distinguished because the female has a strongly pointed abdomen while that of the male is clubbed. After mating, the females jab their pointed tails into the ground to lay their eggs. Altogether, a female common crane-fly will lay about 300 eggs in summer and early autumn.

Liquid food

The larvae of many crane-fly species live in wet soil and in the mud in and around ponds, where they feed on various kinds of decaying material or other insects. However, the larvae of the larger, more familiar species are herbivores. These maggot-like creatures are the notorious leatherjackets, which live in the soil and damage plant roots with their powerful jaws. Up to about 4cm (1⅛in) long with a tough, greyish skin, a leatherjacket drives itself through the soil with a muscular wriggling action. A rosette of fleshy tentacles surrounds the rear end of its body, but it has no legs.

IDENTIFYING CRANE-FLIES

A prominent, V-shaped notch located on the thorax distinguishes crane-flies from similar insects such as midges and mosquitoes. All crane-flies also have a more or less circular cell near the tip of each wing. The hindmost wing vein is long and almost straight.

Identifying individual species is not easy, although the giant crane-fly and spotted crane-fly are distinctive. The smaller *Tipula* species are very alike, but the common crane-fly has longer wings and the first three segments of its antennae are reddish brown. In the marsh crane-fly, only the first two segments are this colour.

◄ All kinds of predators feast on crane-flies, which often die before they get the chance to breed. This one has been trapped by an insect-eating sundew plant.

DISTINCTIVE CRANE-FLIES

Most crane-flies are drably coloured, but *Ctenophora ornata* is one exception. The male, with its yellow abdomen and ornately plumed antennae, is distinctly flamboyant. This species is now quite rare and is included in the *Red Data Book* of endangered species. The larva lives in decaying timber.

The giant crane-fly *Tipula maxima* is not exactly colourful, but as the largest of British crane-flies it is certainly an impressive and even alarming insect. Easily recognised by its size and the large, brown blotches on its wings, it breeds in damp soil in woods and on pond and stream margins.

The name *Ctenophora* is derived from the Latin *cteno*, meaning comb. This refers to the male's feathery antennae.

▲ A crane-fly will sometimes settle on fruit or other juicy foods, as much to lap up moisture as to feed. Its mouthparts are very simple, so it cannot bite or chew.

Spotted crane-fly leatherjackets usually live in flower beds and vegetable plots, chewing through plant roots and often coming to the surface on damp nights to nibble through the stems of young plants. The larvae of the *Tipula* species usually live under grass, and they can cause a lot of damage to meadows, grazing pastures and even cereal crops. They can be a serious pest of park lawns and playing fields, where they create bare patches by killing the grass.

Mating swarms

Leatherjackets spend nearly a year in the ground before turning into pupae. About a fortnight later, the fully developed pupae wriggle to the surface, aided by circles of backward-pointing spines. The cases split open, and the adult flies emerge.

In a productive year – which for crane-flies means a damp one – thousands of adults hatch together, especially in late summer and autumn. When they emerge, many of the smaller crane-flies form huge swarms, in which hundreds or thousands of individuals dance up and down for an hour or more. The insects usually congregate in the late evening, just before sunset, and the swarms consist almost entirely of males. Females are attracted to the dancing masses and are quickly whisked away by the males for mating. The larger species do not swarm in the same way, although they can emerge in such large numbers that they almost seem like swarms.

Once they have mated, crane-flies do not live long. The sole function of the winged adult is to mate and, if female, lay eggs, so adult crane-flies do not eat much, if at all. They can soak up liquid food such as nectar or fruit juices using the fleshy, sponge-like structures at the ends of their snouts, but they rely heavily on energy stored up when they were feeding underground as hungry larvae.

▲ Leatherjackets are not a welcome sight to gardeners. These larval crane-flies, which can be up to about 2cm (¾in) long, spend several months buried in the soil, chewing at the roots of grass and other plants.

◄ Crane-flies mate among vegetation where they are relatively safe from predators. Mating pairs often remain joined together for some time, since this helps the male ensure that the eggs carry his genes.

WILDLIFE WATCH

Where can I see craneflies?

● Long grass and vegetation near lawns and sports fields often harbour crane-flies. Adults often fly in large numbers in early autumn.

● Check garden vegetable plots and flower beds for the spotted crane-fly. The yellow and black markings on the body make it easy to identify.

● If possible, dig beneath bare patches of grass to expose the burrowing larvae, or leatherjackets. These gnaw through the grass roots, killing the plants.

Willowherbs

On warm autumn days, the fluffy white seedheads of many willowherbs open out to catch the breeze and are soon wafted away to colonise damp ground.

Most willowherbs are still in flower in early autumn but as the season progresses their blooms give way to fluffy seedheads. Willowherbs belong to the family Onagraceae, members of which are readily identified by their oval or spear-shaped leaves, pinkish flowers with four notched petals, and long, narrow fruits. Rosebay willowherb and great willowherb are recognised at a glance, but individual species can be more difficult to distinguish. This is mainly because of the confusing array of hybrids that result from interbreeding.

Some 200 species of willowherb grow worldwide, mostly in temperate America and New Zealand. Of the 15 British species, 10 are native. These, and the five introduced species, are all perennial, although they can seem like annuals when they grow and flower rapidly from seed in gardens. Most willowherb species also spread vigorously by means of runners.

Clusters of colour

Willowherbs take their name from their long, narrow leaves, which resemble those of the willow tree. Undivided and variably toothed, they are mostly arranged in opposite pairs. The flowers are borne in loose clusters that vary somewhat in size.

American willowherb has large flower clusters, while the two native upland species, alpine willowherb and chickweed willowherb, have few flowers. The introduced New Zealand willowherb and two similar garden escapes (rockery willowherb and bronzy willowherb) have solitary flowers.

Each flower has four green, narrow, pointed sepals positioned below four purplish pink – sometimes reddish pink or white – petals, eight male stamens and a long female ovary that is divided into four compartments. The cream or whitish female stigma is either four-lobed or club-shaped, providing a useful clue to identification.

After pollination, the ovary ripens into a narrow seed pod up to 10cm (4in) or more long. When ripe the pod splits lengthwise to release numerous seeds, each of which has a tuft of long, white hairs to aid wind dispersal.

Plant invaders

Willowherbs are great colonists of open or previously dug ground, aided by their wind-borne seeds. Rosebay willowherb spread rapidly after the Second World War, because it thrived on bomb-damaged land. One of its alternative common names is 'fireweed', reflecting its affinity for land that has been cleared by fire.

American willowherb, first found in Britain in 1891, is now widespread, including in Ireland. Almost unknown there just 20 years ago, today it occurs over much of the island. New Zealand willowherb is also spreading in mountainous and western areas of Britain and Ireland.

In autumn the white downy seedheads of rosebay willowherb are a common sight on waste ground throughout the British Isles.

DID YOU KNOW?

Native peoples in North America used the tough stem fibres of rosebay willowherb for twine and fishing nets. They also used the young shoots for food and the roots as a medicinal poultice.

A popular name for great willowherb is 'codlins and cream'. This probably derives from the petals, which are rosy pink on top, rather like codlins or cooking apples, and touched with creamy white beneath.

Hoary willowherb or small-flowered hairy willowherb
Epilobium parviflorum

Great willowherb forms dense stands of colour on damp ground alongside rivers, marshes and ditches from July to September.

Great willowherb or codlins and cream
Epilobium hirsutum

WILLOWHERB FACT FILE

● **Great willowherb or codlins and cream**
Epilobium hirsutum
Habitat and distribution
Common in damp or wet places and wasteland; widespread throughout the British Isles, except northern Scotland, where it is rare
Size 100–200cm (3ft 4in–6ft 8in)
Key features
A robust, erect perennial, forming dense stands; stems hairy; leaves in opposite pairs, spear-shaped or oblong, toothed, half-clasping stem; large flowers purplish pink, petals 15–23mm (⅝–⅞in) across, 4-lobed central female stigma; fruits downy, up to 8cm (3in) long
Flowering time
July–September

● **Hoary willowherb or small-flowered hairy willowherb**
Epilobium parviflorum
Habitat and distribution
Widespread in marshy places and waste ground throughout the British Isles, although restricted to east coast in northern Scotland; prefers limey soils
Size 30–80cm (1ft–2ft 8in)
Key features
Similar to great willowherb, but much smaller and less spreading; woolly whitish hairs on lower stem; upper leaves spear-shaped but not opposite or half-clasping; flowers pale purplish pink, petals more deeply notched, 7–12mm (¼–½in) across
Flowering time
July–September

WILLOWHERB FACT FILE

● Broad-leaved willowherb
Epilobium montanum

Habitat and distribution
Common in shady spots in open woods, hedges, waste ground and gardens

Size 20–80cm (8–32in)

Key features
An almost hairless perennial, with rounded stems and clusters of leaf-rosettes in autumn; leaves mostly in opposite pairs, broadly spear-shaped, shallowly toothed; flowers purplish pink, petals deeply notched, 12–15mm (½–⅝in) across, 4-lobed central female stigma; fruits slightly downy, up to 8cm (3in) long

Flowering time
June–September

● Spear-leaved willowherb
Epilobium lanceolatum

Habitat and distribution
Introduced, occurs patchily in dry, open sites as well as churchyards in southern Britain

Size 30–80cm (1ft–2ft 8in)

Key features
Similar to broad-leaved willowherb, but leaves oblong and blunter, stalks up to 1cm (⅜in); upper leaves not opposite; flowers whitish to pale purplish pink

Flowering time
July–September

● American willowherb
Epilobium ciliatum

Habitat and distribution
Widespread in open woods, gardens and waste ground; rare in northern Scotland except on some coasts

Size 20–150cm (8–60in)

Key features
An often reddish stemmed perennial, with 2–4 bristly, raised lines running down stem and many sticky hairs; leaves short-stalked, narrowly spear-shaped, toothed; flowers purplish pink, petals deeply notched with gaps between them, club-shaped central female stigma, 8–10mm (⅜in) across

Flowering time
June–August

● Short-fruited willowherb
Epilobium obscurum

Habitat and distribution
Widespread in woodland edges and damp places

Size 30–90cm (1–3ft)

Key features
A perennial with leafy runners and 4 raised lines running down stem; leaves in opposite pairs, stalkless, narrowly oval to spear-shaped, finely toothed; flowers purplish pink, petals shallowly notched, club-shaped central female stigma, 7–9mm (¼–⅜in) across; fruits only 4–6cm (1½–2½in) long, nearly straight

Flowering time
July–August

● Pale willowherb
Epilobium roseum

Habitat and distribution
Scattered in damp, open woodlands, waste ground and gardens; prefers shade

Size 30–80cm (1ft–2ft 8in)

Key features
Similar to short-fruited willowherb but greyer, without runners and with stalked, more elliptical leaves; flowers white then turning pale pink, about 8–10mm (⅜in) across

Flowering time
July–September

● Square-stemmed willowherb
Epilobium tetragonum

Habitat and distribution
Widespread on damper soils of open woods, hedgerows, waste ground and gardens north to east Yorkshire; rare in Ireland

Size 30–100cm (1ft–3ft 4in)

Key features
Similar to short-fruited willowherb but without runners, with distinctly square stems and longer, more strap-shaped leaves; fruits 7–10cm (2¾–4in) long

Flowering time
July–September

● New Zealand willowherb
Epilobium brunnescens

Habitat and distribution
Introduced, common in some places on streamsides and in wet, gravelly places in the north and west

Size 5–10cm (2–4in)

Key features
A low-growing perennial with mats of slender, prostrate stems; roots readily; leaves purplish beneath, finely toothed, oval, less than 1cm (⅜in) long, short-stalked; flowers pale pink-whitish, solitary, up to 6mm (¼in) across; fruits dark red, 2–3cm (¾–1¼in) long

Flowering time
May–October

● Rockery willowherb
Epilobium pedunculare

Similar to New Zealand willowherb but with bigger, rounder, sharper-toothed leaves that are not purple beneath; rock-garden escape, especially in western Ireland

● Bronzy willowherb
Epilobium komarovianum

Similar to rockery willowherb but with untoothed elliptical leaves; rock-garden escape in scattered sites in Ireland

American willowherb
Epilobium ciliatum

Broad-leaved willowherb
Epilobium montanum

Spear-leaved willowherb
Epilobium lanceolatum

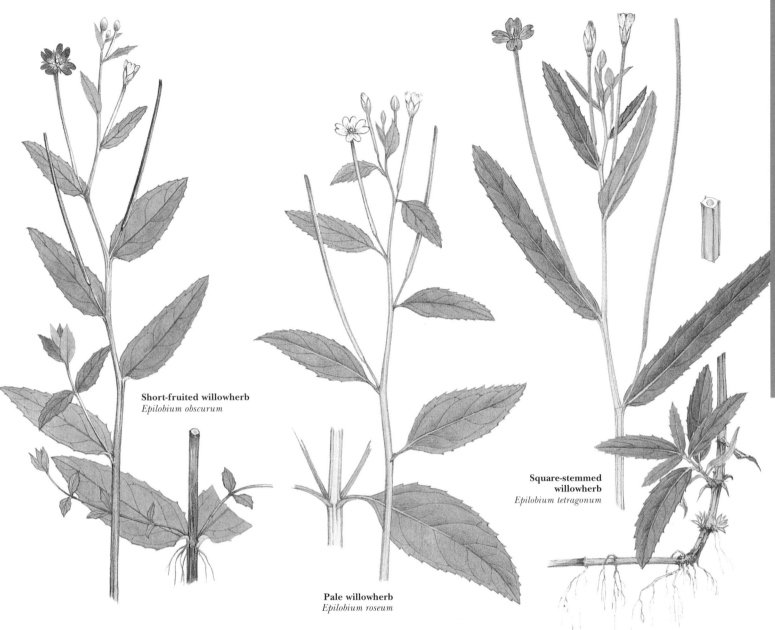

Short-fruited willowherb
Epilobium obscurum

Pale willowherb
Epilobium roseum

Square-stemmed willowherb
Epilobium tetragonum

New Zealand willowherb
Epilobium brunnescens

Broad-leaved willowherb
is abundant throughout
Britain and Ireland,
swathing woodlands,
walls and hedge banks in
purplish pink from June
to September.

WILLOWHERB FACT FILE

● **Alpine willowherb**
Epilobium anagallidifolium
Habitat and distribution
Common in some wet, mossy places in mountains of northern Britain
Size 5–15cm (2–6in)
Key features
A low-growing perennial with slender, prostrate and erect reddish stems; leaves yellow-green, oval or elliptical, little-toothed, in opposite pairs, short-stalked; flowers pinkish with reddish sepals, 7–10mm (¼–⅜in) across; fruits dark red, up to 3.5cm (1⅜in) long
Flowering time
July–August

● **Chickweed willowherb**
Epilobium alsinifolium
Habitat and distribution
Common by streams in the mountains of northern Britain and in one area of north-west Ireland around County Leitrim
Size 10–25cm (4–10in)
Key features
Similar to alpine willowherb but less slender, with runners and larger, more toothed bluish-green leaves; flowers 14–16mm (⅝–¾in) across
Flowering time
July–September

● **Rosebay willowherb or fireweed**
Chamerion angustifolium
Habitat and distribution
Common on heaths and mountains and especially waste ground; more scattered in Ireland
Size 100–180cm (3ft 4in–6ft) tall
Key features
An erect, leafy, almost hairless perennial, forms dense stands; leaves narrowly spear-shaped, pointed, spiral along stem; flowers bright purplish pink, in a long spike, 20–30mm (¾–1¼in) across; fruits downy, up to 10cm (4in) long
Flowering time
June–September

● **Marsh willowherb**
Epilobium palustre
Habitat and distribution
Common in marshes, bogs and wet woodland clearings on acid soils
Size Up to 60cm (2ft) tall
Key features
A slender perennial with mostly underground runners; leaves mostly in opposite pairs, stalkless, narrowly spear-shaped, sparsely toothed, bluish green; flowers pale pink or whitish, club-shaped central female stigma, about 13mm (⅝in) across
Flowering time
June–August

Rosebay willowherb or fireweed
Chamerion angustifolium

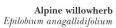

Alpine willowherb
Epilobium anagallidifolium

Marsh willowherb
Epilobium palustre

Chickweed willowherb
Epilobium alsinifolium

WILDLIFE WATCH

Where can I see willowherbs ?

● Most willowherbs are plants of damp, open woods and hedgerows, parkland, overgrown cemeteries, waysides and disturbed or cultivated land. Broad-leaved willowherb, in particular, is a parkland and garden weed.

● Three species occur in upland areas – alpine and chickweed willowherb grow in damp, mossy places, while New Zealand willowherb favours many types of damp, bare ground from peaty moorland to railway verges.

Recognising shrubs and small trees

Parks and roadsides are often scattered with shrubs and small trees, many of which are unremarkable for most of the year. In autumn, however, they may be laden with colourful fruits and exhibit distinctive twigs and leaves.

Mature woodland trees are perhaps the most conspicuous natural features of the landscape, but in autumn, the smaller shrubs and trees come into their own. Not only do they display colourful foliage, but they are often densely covered with attractive red, pink, yellow or black fruits.

Autumn fruits

Fruit-producing trees and shrubs belong to several plant families, including the Rosaceae (rose) and Caprifoliaceae (honeysuckle) families. They tend to grow in copses and hedgerows, and along waysides. Unlike the larger woodland trees, many of which produce wind-pollinated flowers in early spring, their flowers are mostly insect-pollinated. The need to attract insects means the flowers are often fragrant and conspicuous, borne in large clusters, and produced in spring or early summer. Once pollinated, the developing seeds are enclosed within an ovary, which ripens to form a fleshy, colourful fruit.

The most common type of hedgerow fruit is the berry, a term often used loosely to describe any fleshy fruit, but strictly a fruit containing several seeds. Another common type is the drupe – a single-seeded fleshy fruit, as produced by blackthorn and other wild plums. The fruits of some plants in the rose family are called berries although they have a more complex structure. For example, a single blackberry is actually a cluster of small drupes or 'drupelets'. The crab apple is yet another type

Wild, straggly branches and a short trunk characterise the crab apple tree. Its small golden fruits are sour to human tastebuds, but relished by birds.

of fruit, known botanically as a 'pome'. The apple forms by the base, or receptacle, of the flower swelling to surround the ripening seeds. The rosehip has a similar but looser structure.

Winter provisions

As well as being highly decorative, the bright colouring of these autumn fruits serves a serious purpose. Birds and small mammals are enticed to feed upon them, later dispersing the seeds. Nourishment from this autumn feast is vitally

important to many wild animals, enabling them to survive the coming winter.

Some berries can be eaten by humans, but many are bitter and unpalatable and some are poisonous. Others have medicinal uses, but only in the hands of a trained herbalist. With a few exceptions, such as, in some cases, ivy, yew and spindle, the berries do not harm birds, and native species as well as winter visitors such as fieldfares and redwings – even waxwings in some years – gorge themselves on the autumn bounty of the hedgerows.

EASY GUIDE TO SPOTTING SHRUBS AND SMALL TREES

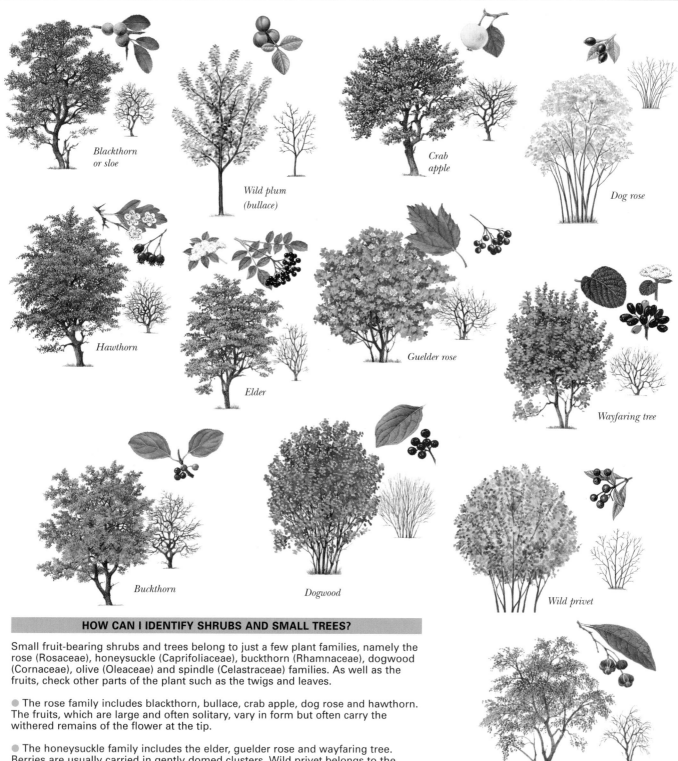

Blackthorn or sloe

Wild plum (bullace)

Crab apple

Dog rose

Hawthorn

Elder

Guelder rose

Wayfaring tree

Buckthorn

Dogwood

Wild privet

Spindle

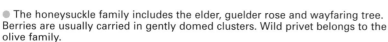

HOW CAN I IDENTIFY SHRUBS AND SMALL TREES?

Small fruit-bearing shrubs and trees belong to just a few plant families, namely the rose (Rosaceae), honeysuckle (Caprifoliaceae), buckthorn (Rhamnaceae), dogwood (Cornaceae), olive (Oleaceae) and spindle (Celastraceae) families. As well as the fruits, check other parts of the plant such as the twigs and leaves.

● The rose family includes blackthorn, bullace, crab apple, dog rose and hawthorn. The fruits, which are large and often solitary, vary in form but often carry the withered remains of the flower at the tip.

● The honeysuckle family includes the elder, guelder rose and wayfaring tree. Berries are usually carried in gently domed clusters. Wild privet belongs to the olive family.

● Buckthorn, dogwood and wild privet all have clusters of spherical black fruits. Alder buckthorn has thinner branches than buckthorn, untoothed leaves and no thorns.

● The spindle has coral-pink fruits that split to reveal bright orange seeds.

◄ The berries of alder buckthorn ripen from red to black much like those of buckthorn. In both plants the berries are poisonous, but much more so in alder buckthorn.

DANGER!

As with fungi, never cook or eat the fruits of wild shrubs or trees unless you are absolutely confident about their identity. Many are poisonous.

BLACKTHORN OR SLOE *Prunus spinosa*

In March and April, the conspicuous white, five-petalled flowers blanket the countryside like snow, giving rise to the description 'blackthorn winter'. The plum-like fruits are used to make sloe gin.

Sloe comes from the Anglo-Saxon word 'slah', which means bluish.

● **SIZE**
Shrub or small tree up to 4m (13ft) tall

● **TWIGS AND LEAVES**
Twigs thorny, downy when young, later greyish or blackish brown; leaves oval, blunt, minutely toothed, hairless, green or yellowish in autumn. White flowers appear in spring before the leaves

● **FRUITS**
Miniature, rounded plums, blackish with a bluish grey bloom; flesh green and sour

● **HABITAT AND DISTRIBUTION**
A major shrub of hedgerows and woodland margins; forms impenetrable thickets on chalk downs, sea cliffs and shingle beaches; common everywhere except northern Scotland

WILD PLUM (BULLACE) *Prunus domestica*

This subspecies of wild plum has globular fruits, but it is very variable as it interbreeds with other wild plums, such as damson and greengage. The white April flowers are often mistaken for blackthorn.

The fruits of wild plum are usually purple but can be pink or yellow.

● **SIZE**
Shrub or small tree up to 10m (33ft) tall

● **TWIGS AND LEAVES**
The twigs are rather thorny, downy when young, becoming grey or brown; leaves oval, larger than those of sloe, downy, minutely toothed, yellow in autumn

● **FRUITS**
Small plums a little larger than sloes; flesh green and usually sour but sometimes sweeter, depending on interbreeding

● **HABITAT AND DISTRIBUTION**
A shrub of hedgerows, especially around villages and former settlements; rare in Scotland and western and northern Ireland

CRAB APPLE *Malus sylvestris*

The wild crab apple tree is small and spiny, with leaves that are hairless when mature. A native tree, the crab apple is widely used as rootstock for grafting.

Rosy and tempting, crab apples are bitter to taste, but relished by thrushes.

● **SIZE**
Small tree up to 10m (33ft) tall

● **TWIGS AND LEAVES**
The twigs are thorny, reddish brown; leaves oval with a pointed tip, toothed, downy when young, hairless and yellow in autumn

● **FRUITS**
Miniature apples up to about 3cm (1¼in) across, usually yellow, sometimes reddish, with hard, sour flesh

● **HABITAT AND DISTRIBUTION**
Widespread and sometimes frequent in woods and hedges; often grows alongside main roads; rare in Scotland

DOG ROSE *Rosa canina*

A rambling plant of hedgerows, the dog rose has bright red fruits known as 'hips'. It is one of the most common of several similar wild roses.

The autumn fruits of the dog rose are a rich source of vitamin C. They are used in teas, jams and syrups.

● **SIZE**
Sprawling shrub with long, arching stems and branches

● **TWIGS AND LEAVES**
Twigs reddish brown, covered with stout, curved prickles; leaves compound with toothed oval leaflets, downy beneath, falling early in autumn

● **FRUITS**
Egg or flask-shaped, red or scarlet 'hips'

● **HABITAT AND DISTRIBUTION**
Widespread and sometimes frequent in hedges, but less common in northern England, Scotland and Ireland

HAWTHORN *Crataegus monogyna*

As well as being a hedgerow shrub, hawthorn is also a woodland tree. In spring the massed white flowers release a strong scent, while in autumn the bright red fruits make an impressive display.

Hawthorn berries, or 'haws', are a major source of food for wild birds.

● **SIZE**
Shrub or small tree up to 15m (50ft) tall

● **TWIGS AND LEAVES**
Twigs thorny, reddish brown; leaves oval, deeply cut into toothed lobes, tawny to red in autumn

● **FRUITS**
Almost spherical, dull red berries, each one containing a single seed, with a single style protruding from the tip of the fruit

● **HABITAT AND DISTRIBUTION**
Common throughout the British Isles, planted widely since the 18th century; also grows in woodland and dense scrub, especially in hilly areas and near the sea. The related Midland or woodland hawthorn (*Crataegus laevigata*) is generally scarcer and absent from northern England, Scotland and Ireland

ELDER *Sambucus nigra*

Much folklore has grown up around elder. It has long been used in herbal medicine and even during the 20th century hedge-cutters would spare elder out of respect for its magical powers.

Elderberries are used in teas and cordials to help to fight colds and flu.

● **SIZE**
Shrub or small tree up to 10m (33ft) tall

● **TWIGS AND LEAVES**
Twigs green, becoming brown and corky with white pith; leaves compound with broadly spear-shaped, toothed leaflets, green or reddish in autumn

● **FRUITS**
Wide, flat clusters of small, black (rarely greenish), glossy berries

● **HABITAT AND DISTRIBUTION**
Common throughout the British Isles, except in the higher mountains; often seen where the soil has been enriched, such as around farms, gardens and human habitation; also near rabbit warrens (rabbits do not eat it)

GUELDER ROSE *Viburnum opulus*

This attractive shrub is found in damp, scrubby places, and is also cultivated. The maple-like leaves are an unusual and conspicuous feature. White flowers appear in June and July.

The round, glistening berries of guelder rose are almost translucent.

● **SIZE**
Large, robust shrub 2–4m (6½–13ft) tall

● **TWIGS AND LEAVES**
Twigs greyish, hairless; leaves 3 to 5-lobed, almost hairless, turn dull crimson in autumn

● **FRUITS**
Clusters of red, glossy, rather waxy berries; inedible, often remain after leaves have fallen

● **HABITAT AND DISTRIBUTION**
Widespread in damp woods, hedges and fens, beside rivers and streams; more localised in Scotland and much of Ireland

WAYFARING TREE *Viburnum lantana*

A feature of hedges in some districts with lime-rich soils, this plant is closely related to many garden viburnums. The cream-white flowers appear from late April to June.

The berries, held in large, flat-topped clusters, ripen from red to black at different times.

● **SIZE**
Fairly thorny shrub up to 6m (20ft) tall

● **TWIGS AND LEAVES**
Twigs blackish or greyish; leaves oval, blunt, finely toothed, yellow or brown in autumn

● **FRUITS**
Clusters of small, oval, red then black, glossy berries borne in a flat head; poisonous

● **HABITAT AND DISTRIBUTION**
Sometimes common on chalk and limestone and in fens in England as far north as southern Lancashire and Yorkshire; also found in southern Scotland; rarer in Ireland; native only in southern England but has been planted on roadside verges, which has influenced the plant's distribution

BUCKTHORN *Rhamnus cathartica*

This shrub or small tree grows in hedgerows and woods and is laden with black berries in autumn. The tiny greenish flowers appear in May to June.

Male and female flowers grow on separate trees, berries appearing only on the female trees.

● **SIZE**
Dense, thorny shrub up to 8m (26ft) tall

● **TWIGS AND LEAVES**
Twigs blackish or greyish, thorny; leaves oval, blunt, finely toothed, yellow or brown in autumn

● **FRUITS**
Clusters of small, black, glossy berries; poisonous

● **HABITAT AND DISTRIBUTION**
Sometimes common on chalk and limestone and in fens northwards to Cumbria, especially in central and southern England; rarer in Ireland

DOGWOOD *Cornus sanguinea*

Dogwood's crimson winter twigs are its most distinctive feature, more noteworthy than the pale cream flowers that appear in midsummer or the small black berries in autumn.

Large, flat-topped heads of creamy-white flowers are popular with insects.

● **SIZE**
Upright shrub, 1–4m (3–13ft) tall

● **TWIGS AND LEAVES**
Twigs crimson in winter and smooth; leaves in opposite pairs, oval pointed, with 3–5 prominent veins; red in autumn

● **FRUITS**
Clusters of globular, purplish black drupes; poisonous

● **HABITAT AND DISTRIBUTION**
Common in scrub and hedges on chalk and limestone in much of Britain, especially central and southern regions; occurs locally in central and western Ireland

WILD PRIVET *Ligustrum vulgare*

Clusters of scented white flowers appear in June and July followed by black berries, which are similar to those of buckthorn. Wild privet is one of Britain's few native evergreens.

The berries of wild privet were once crushed to produce a blue-black dye.

● **SIZE**
Many-branched, evergreen shrub, 1–3m (3–10ft) tall

● **TWIGS AND LEAVES**
Twigs downy, leaves spear-shaped, pointed, toothed, hairless, remaining dark green in autumn but may turn bronze in winter

● **FRUITS**
Clusters of small, black, glossy berries; poisonous

● **HABITAT AND DISTRIBUTION**
Widespread in scrub mainly on lime-rich soils, in southern England and south Wales and most of Ireland; scarcer in north of Britain; sometimes planted in garden hedges, although the usual privet of hedges is the more robust Japanese species, *Ligustrum japonicum*

SPINDLE *Euonymus europaeus*

So named because its wood was used to make spindles for weaving, this plant is one of the glories of autumn, with its colourful fruits and leaves. Inconspicuous, small cream flowers appear in June.

Spindle's coral-pink fruits are relished by garden birds, especially robins.

● **SIZE**
A slender shrub or small tree up to 6m (20ft) tall

● **TWIGS AND LEAVES**
Twigs more or less square in section, smooth green; leaves elliptical or broadly spear-shaped, pointed, finely toothed, hairless, dark red in autumn

● **FRUITS**
4-lobed, matt pink capsules that split into segments to reveal 4 orange seeds; poisonous

● **HABITAT AND DISTRIBUTION**
Widespread in hedges and woods, especially on chalk and limestone in southern England; less so in northern England, Wales and Ireland; absent from Scotland except for south-east

Index

Wildlife Watch
Gardens & Parks in Autumn

Published by the Reader's Digest Association Limited, 2006

The Reader's Digest Association Limited
11 Westferry Circus, Canary Wharf
London E14 4HE

We are committed to both the quality of our products and the service we provide to our customers, so please feel free to contact us on 08705 113366, or via our website at: www.readersdigest.co.uk

If you have any comments about the content of our books you can contact us at: gbeditorial@readersdigest.co.uk

® Reader's Digest, The Digest and the Pegasus logo are registered trademarks of The Reader's Digest Association, Inc., of Pleasantville, New York, USA

Reader's Digest General Books:
Editorial Director   Julian Browne
Art Director   Nick Clark
Series Editor   Christine Noble
Project Editor   Lisa Thomas
Project Art Editor   Julie Bennett
Prepress Accounts Manager   Penelope Grose

This book was designed, edited and produced by Eaglemoss Publications Ltd, based on material first published as the partwork *Wildlife of Britain*

For Eaglemoss:
Project Editor   Marion Paull
Editors   Paul Brewer, Celia Coyne, Samantha Gray, John Woodward
Art Editor   Phil Gibbs
Editorial Assistant   Helen Hawksfield
Consultant   Jonathan Elphick

Publishing Manager   Nina Hathway

CONCEPT CODE: UK 0133/G/S
BOOK CODE: 630-012
ISBN: 0 276 44060 9
ORACLE CODE: 356200005H.00.24